D1554955

The Unofficial Diplomat

Memoirs and Occasional Papers
Association for Diplomatic Studies and Training

In 2003, the Association for Diplomatic Studies and Training (ADST) created the Memoirs and Occasional Papers Series to preserve firsthand accounts and other informed observations on foreign affairs for scholars, journalists, and the general public. Sponsoring publication of the series is one of numerous ways in which ADST, a nonprofit organization founded in 1986, seeks to promote understanding of American diplomacy and those who conduct it. Together with the Foreign Affairs Oral History program and ADST's support for the training of foreign affairs personnel at the State Department's Foreign Service Institute, these efforts constitute the Association's fundamental purposes.

J. Chapman Chester, *FROM FOGGY BOTTOM TO CAPITOL HILL*
Exploits of a G.I., Diplomat, and Congressional Aide

John Gunther Dean, *DANGER ZONES*
A Diplomat's Fight for America's Interests

Robert E. Gribbin, *IN THE AFTERMATH OF GENOCIDE*
The U.S. Role in Rwanda

Allen C. Hansen, *NINE LIVES*
A Foreign Service Odyssey

James R. Huntley, *AN ARCHITECT OF DEMOCRACY*
Building a Mosaic of Peace

John G. Kormann, *ECHOES OF A DISTANT CLARION*
Recollections of a Diplomat and Soldier

Armin Meyer, *QUIET DIPLOMACY*
From Cairo to Tokyo in the Twilight of Imperialism

William Morgan and Charles Stuart Kennedy, eds., *AMERICAN DIPLOMATS*
The Foreign Service at Work

James M. Potts
FRENCH COVERT ACTION IN THE AMERICAN REVOLUTION

Howard L. Steele, *BUSHELS AND BALES*
A Food Soldier in the Cold War

Daniel Whitman, *A HAITI CHRONICLE*
The Undoing of a Latent Democracy

The Unofficial Diplomat

A Memoir

by Joanne Grady Huskey

Association for Diplomatic Studies and Training
Memoirs and Occasional Papers Series

NEW ACADEMIA PUBLISHING   SCARITH

Washington, DC

Copyright © Joanne Grady Huskey, 2009

The views and opinions in this book are solely those of the author and not necessarily those of the Association for Diplomatic Studies and Training or the United States Government.

New Academia Publishing/SCARITH Books, 2009

All rights reserved. No part of this book may be reproduced or transmitted in any form or by any means, electronic or mechanical, including photocopying, recording, or by any information storage and retrieval system.

Printed in the United States of America

Library of Congress Control Number: 2009931654
ISBN 978-0-9823867-2-9 paperback (alk. paper)

 An imprint of New Academia Publishing
P.O. Box 27420, Washington, DC 20038-7420

 NEW ACADEMIA
PUBLISHING
www.newacademia.com
info@newacademia.com

This book is dedicated to my loving husband, Jim Huskey, who has always given me support and encouragement and without whom these life adventures would not have been possible.

We must focus our energies beyond the guns and steel of the military. We must focus our energies on the other elements of national power that will be so crucial in the years to come. The military is no replacement for civilian involvement and expertise. Where civilians are on the ground, even in small numbers, we have seen tangible and often dramatic changes.

Robert Gates, Secretary of Defense,
at Kansas State University
November 2007

In today's world, we need not only the professional diplomats who serve in our foreign services and represent our country to one another. We need the citizen diplomats who realize that there is no escape. We are in this together. We may have profound differences, but I am often reminded that as we learn more from science about the human genome, we recognize that we are 99.9 percent the same. As you look at our DNA, you don't see religion or race; you see humanity.

Hillary Clinton, Secretary of State
New Delhi, India
July 20th, 2009

Contents

Prologue

Staring at Charlie Chaplain's foot and handprints, as they filled with water in the pouring rain on the sidewalk in front of Grauman's Chinese Theater in Los Angeles, anticipation swelled within me. It seemed a most unlikely place to meet Lu Yong, my Chinese teacher, whom I hadn't seen in the dozen years since leaving Beijing in 1991. So much had happened in both of our lives; we had both traveled all over the world.

It was 2003 and I had been back in the States for almost three years. It seemed inconceivable that my friend Lu Yong was now living in Los Angeles, married with two children—"made in America" of all things—and operating his own travel agency and ship supply business. In his travel agency, his clients were mostly Chinese tourists, and most of them wanted to see Disneyland, Universal Studios, and MGM. Was this really the same Lu Yong I had known so long ago in a very different China? Meanwhile, China had changed, so had I, and so presumably had Lu Yong.

Quintessentially American, California was unknown territory for our children, Christopher and Caroline, who—although American by birth—had spent little time in the United States, because my husband, Jim, and I had lived overseas for the previous decade. Spring break from school seemed the perfect opportunity to drive them up the West Coast. Our first stop was L.A., that haven of the glitziest aspects of American culture. After some detective work, I finally tracked down Lu Yong and called him. Quite shocked but delighted to hear my voice, he exclaimed, "I can't believe it's you, Zhou An Na! Let me take your family on the Grand Tour of Los

Angeles! I'll treat you. I have passes to Disneyland and Universal Studios. Where do you want to meet?"

It seemed appropriate to meet at Grauman's Chinese Theater on Hollywood Boulevard in downtown L.A., since Lu Yong had been my guide through China during those chaotic days in Beijing. Amazingly, he was now able to offer the same kindness to my American children, guiding them through a part of their own country they had yet to discover.

Out of the jostling crowd standing in the rain, a familiar, almost shy smile transported me back to twelve years earlier.

There stood Lu Yong, as reliable as ever, offering cover from the torrential rains, in what we had expected to be sunny southern California. His face looked the same, though a bit older and more serious. While his clothes were more stylish than those he wore in China, and his teeth had been repaired, leaving no sign of the earlier decay, our connection remained as solid as ever.

After he showed us the movie stars' footprints, we all hopped into his large new SUV, a far cry from the old black clunker bicycle he rode in Beijing. Driving north into the foothills to Universal Studios, he flashed his pass and opened the gates of one of America's favorite fantasylands. Twelve-year-old Christopher immediately gravitated toward the Hard Rock Cafe, and before we knew it, we were eating lunch next to Kurt Cobain's and Jimi Hendrix's Stratocaster guitars. It was there, in that most unlikely place, that Lu Yong shared with us the amazing tale of what had happened to him after we parted in Beijing in 1991.

In the late summer of 1991, I had frantically searched for Lu Yong to say goodbye before we left Beijing, but he was nowhere to be found. None of his friends knew where he was either. At the time, I feared it might have been because we were unable to help him get a visa to leave China. This left me very sad, because Lu Yong had been one of my closest Chinese friends, and we had gone through so much together. It was extremely odd that he had not even come to say goodbye to us.

On that day, twelve years later in Los Angeles, he told Jim and me that the reason he could not come to say farewell was because the Chinese security police had arrested him and thrown him into prison. His crime was associating too closely with Americans, me in particular. For six months, he was kept in a cold, dank Beijing prison, while guards harassed and interrogated him daily for information about the U.S. embassy and how it functioned. They finally released him after he signed a "confession" admitting that he had committed a crime against his country by associating with Americans during the time of the Tiananmen Square demonstrations in the spring of 1989.

After his release from jail, the deeply distrustful Lu Yong slipped aboard a train headed for the Soviet Union and escaped to Europe with the aim of marrying an Italian girlfriend. By the time my family had moved to Madras, India, in 1993, he had made his way to Italy to find his girlfriend, who much to his surprise was already married to a rich Italian husband, and wasn't too pleased to see Lu Yong. For several years he shuttled between Italy and Czechoslovakia trying to start an import/export business. By 1996, he reached his long-sought goal—the United States. In 1998, during his early months in the United States, he was shocked when he saw news broadcasts showing our family in Kenya after the bombing of the American Embassy; but that proved to be his means of tracking us down. By the time we moved back to the States, he had reunited with his long-lost Chinese girlfriend, married, and established his businesses in Los Angeles.

We were awed by this long saga, amazed that he was sitting there in the Hard Rock Cafe in Los Angeles, able to tell us his incredible story!

Over lunch, we told Lu Yong of our own lives and experiences living in South India and Kenya. After eating, he asked us, "Do you think you'll go overseas again, after all that you have been through?"

"We can't decide," I replied. "On the one hand, the world is changing rapidly, and so many people seem to hate Americans lately. I don't want my family to be caught up in another terrorist attack. On the other hand, we still want to expose our children to the world, so they can understand and appreciate other cultures."

"Well, it took me almost ten years to get to the U.S., and I couldn't be happier," Lu Yong countered.

"But the media announce new terrorist threats every day. It's not that much safer here than overseas. In fact, Washington, D.C., where we live, might be the least safe place in the world right now," I admitted. "Our best bet may be to take our kids abroad once more. After all, if I hadn't moved to China, I would never have met you!"

"Yeah, and I suppose if I hadn't known you, I may never have come to America at all," nodded Lu Yong.

We both smiled, old friends drinking Chinese tea in the Hard Rock Cafe in Los Angeles, while the sights and sounds of Universal studios beckoned us—Chinese and American, changed by having known each other. Such a small world!

1
Beginnings

It all began rather innocently. When I married Jim, we were both living and working in Washington, D.C. We had both lived and traveled overseas on and off for many years. We both had apartments on Capitol Hill and worked across the street from each other, he at the State Department, I at the Kennedy Center. We probably had unknowingly jogged past each other many mornings on the National Mall.

Although we are both Americans, our marriage was a bit like two foreigners getting together. I am a Yankee, with family from New England and New Jersey. Tall and auburn-haired, I was born the eldest in a large Irish Catholic family and went to Catholic parochial schools. I was accustomed to excursions to Manhattan, the Jersey shore, Dairy Queens, and corner delis. I had the usual upbringing of a suburban American girl—piano lessons, dance classes, and Girl Scouts. I attended the University of Wisconsin for my undergraduate studies, majoring in philosophy, and later completed graduate studies in education at Harvard University. Earlier in my career, I had worked in television and the theatre. As the international director of Very Special Arts International, an organization with offices in the John F. Kennedy Center in Washington, I had been working with the Kennedy family for many years. Charged with setting up national arts programs involving disabled people around the world, I had visited forty-five different countries from 1981 to 1985 and forged friendships around the world.

My husband is a tall, sandy-haired Southerner from South Alabama. He grew up as a Southern Baptist, with Bible "sword drills," fish fries, hush puppies, boiled peanuts, and grits. His, too, was a typical American upbringing—baseball, summers at the beach in North Carolina, Eagle Scouts, and college fraternity life. He had broken away from the South and its conservative (then segregationist) mentality. Our paths had previously crossed, although we never met, when he attended graduate school at the University of Wisconsin. He earned a doctorate in American Diplomatic History at the University of North Carolina and hitchhiked around the world for several years in the 1970s, ending up in Hong Kong and Taiwan, where he learned Mandarin. When we met, Jim was working for the U.S. Information Agency (USIA) as a China analyst. He, too, had friends all round the world.

We met at a Christmas party in 1984 at the Dupont Circle home of Louis and Cindy, mutual friends from Saint Mark's Episcopal Church on Capitol Hill. It was a frigid evening, but full of holiday color, holly on the doors, sparkling lights glowing on trees in the windows of old townhouses. Both a bit taller than most, we flirted for much of the party without talking, our eyes connecting above the heads of the crowded living room. It was the arched eyebrows behind his John Lennon-style rimless glasses that first caught my eye. He struck me as a vintage sixties intellectual.

Through the evening, we edged closer and closer, finally ending up face-to-face just as I was about to leave to go to another party. The conversation was comfortable from the start, because of the Wisconsin connection—we figured we had probably been in the same anti–Vietnam War demonstrations on campus and breathed the same acrid tear gas—and our common years of travel. We had traveled to many of the same places in Asia, Africa, and Europe, although he had used his thumb and rickety buses and trains to get around, while I flew in comfort.

"Why are you leaving so soon?" Jim queried.

"I am going to another Christmas party at the home of a friend," I responded.

"I'll take you there," he offered. For whatever reason—because he seemed nice?—I consented. We left that party and, although we barely knew each other, went together to two other parties in Georgetown before the night was finished. It was a long and most interesting evening that didn't end until around three in the morning.

After a year and a half of courting, this northern Catholic girl married that southern Baptist boy and halved the difference by turning Episcopalian. Thinking that we would then finally settle down to a nice quiet life in Washington, we bought a cozy nineteenth-century townhouse on Capitol Hill with white stucco walls, vaulted and beamed ceilings, dark Spanish arches, and a romantic fireplace and sauna in our bedroom. We jogged together down the Mall each morning before going to our respective jobs. Our first year was a whirl of furniture shopping and home decorating in between my travels to Africa, South America, and Asia for work. Thus, happily did we begin our life together in America.

Late one night in August 1987, while on one of my working trips to Asia for the Kennedy Center, Jim called my hotel. Having just arrived in Beijing and weary from thirty-seven hours of traveling, I heard my husband's distant voice ask me cryptically over the phone, "How would you like to *live* in China?"

"What do you mean?" I responded groggily.

"Well, Sweetheart, I've just been offered a place in the fall Foreign Service class at the State Department," he explained. It turned out that, without telling me, he had slipped away one Saturday, under the pretext of a usual trip to Hechinger's hardware store, and taken the Foreign Service exam. He repeated the subterfuge a few months later when he took the oral interview. Now, out of 25,000 applicants who took the test, he and forty-three others had been offered places.

I was jolted awake by his question out of the blue from the other side of the world. I had come to Beijing to work on an arts program with Bette Bao Lord, the wife of Winston Lord, then U.S. ambassador to China. The thought of actually moving to China had never crossed my mind. Jim asked me to take a hard look at the life I saw in China to see if I would like living there. I told him to tell the State Department that his wife was far away, and he couldn't possibly give them an answer on joining the Foreign Service until I got back to discuss it properly. When I returned home a week later, Jim had already turned down the State Department, but it was clear from his depressed demeanor that he was deeply disappointed. We schemed, talked about the future, and finally agreed to give the Foreign Service a try as long as it was also good for *me*.

2

It's Hard Holding Up Half the Sky

Eight months later, we were in Beijing. After nine years at the Kennedy Center, I had quit my job, packed our things, said goodbye to friends and family, and moved to the far side of the world. As Jim was a China specialist and I had some contacts in China, we had succeeded in convincing State Department personnel officers to give us Beijing for our first posting. I suppose we were lucky, given the small and remote posts listed on our first Foreign Service bid list—it could just as easily have been Ouagadougou. We were dreamily excited and ready for the new adventure.

Upon arrival in China, however, we reacted in totally opposite ways. For Jim, who had studied Chinese for years and whose doctoral studies concentrated on U.S.-China relations, it was heaven, a dream come true. When our plane landed for a late-night stopover in Shanghai en route to Beijing, he excitedly rushed off to talk with any Chinese people he could find in the airport transit lounge. In his haste, he left me face-to-face with two machinegun-toting People's Liberation Army (PLA) soldiers making what were clearly rude remarks in Chinese to my face, the gist of which was clear, despite the strange guttural sounds of Chinese. The Shanghai International Airport was dusty and drab, with a low, harsh light and PLA soldiers in dull green uniforms everywhere. Expressionless workers sat behind stands with nothing for sale. The whole scene was lifeless and joyless. It made me feel empty, terrified, and sick to my stomach. What had I done to my life?

When we reboarded our plane to continue our journey to Beijing, Jim turned and, overflowing with excitement, said, "Isn't it fantastic to be here? This is going to be wonderful! I can't believe I am finally here!"

I looked at him, blinking back tears, and finally burst out, "I can't live here! It's so drab and colorless; I feel claustrophobic with soldiers everywhere. I am going to die of sensory deprivation," I whispered, though the lump in my throat was so big, I could barely speak. "I want to turn this plane around and go home now!"

To make matters worse, much worse, when we reached Beijing, no one from the American Embassy was there to meet us at the airport. (We learned later that we had been expected the following day.) With Jim's rusty Chinese, we had to fend for ourselves and find a way into Beijing with our collection of huge suitcases and somehow find a hotel room for the night. The midnight ride into Beijing from the airport for me seemed like something out of an Ingmar Bergman film—bleak and empty. We passed oxcarts loaded with people, bicycles weaving on and off the bumpy road, and the dully egalitarian, nondescript communist-bloc housing. Everything, including my mood, was dark gray. The streets were choked with brown dust, black coal smoke, and throngs of people in dark navy Mao jackets. Somberness hung over everything. Life had been molded to conform to a drab standard of communist grayness. Even the people seemed to me drab, gray, and beaten down.

This was China in 1988—a China, I came to learn, undergoing rapid change. I vowed that I would not let myself be pulled down, and I would start by making our home a haven of color, music, and beauty—a refuge from the drab surrounding world. And I would do a lot of praying.

The first weeks in Beijing were some of the hardest in my life. I felt a huge sense of loss and depression. Surrounded by an insuperable language barrier, I could not speak with any Chinese people beyond the walls of the Jianguo Hotel. The morning after we arrived, Jim went eagerly off to his first Foreign Service posting, at the Embassy three blocks away. I, however, was left alone with my whole life, even my Rolodex, packed in boxes stacked to the ceiling of our hotel room. I felt as if my identity were buried and lost deep in those boxes.

The Jianguo Hotel was one of the few Western-style hotels in the still very closed Beijing of 1988. We were fortunate to get a room there. The hotel was a haven for Westerners. They hung out in the

Garden Coffee Shop, which could have been in New Jersey, and in the bustling, cozy lobby, looking out onto a courtyard of greenery and tropical fish ponds. Western journalists gathered there daily to compare notes, expatriates met there Sundays to listen to Western classical music, and the international community bought fresh French baguettes and dined at the French and Swiss restaurants just off the lobby. I worked off some of my anxieties in a small lap pool in the basement.

After a few days, life seemed survivable, but I wasn't sure that would be enough. We had a two-floor suite, with a small kitchenette and living room on the lower level and a master bedroom upstairs. We lived there for four months with our lives on hold, surrounded by huge airfreight boxes, until our official housing was ready for us. In November, when we were getting ready for the Marine Corps Ball at the Great Wall Sheraton Hotel, we ransacked those huge boxes trying to find Jim's tuxedo. We finally located the tux, but had to improvise for the missing shirt studs and cufflinks. We arrived at the Great Wall Sheraton with Jim looking quite fashionable, with my rhinestone earrings filling in as studs down the front of his tux shirt, my red scarf for a cummerbund, and paper clips for cuff links.

The Jianguo Hotel was a kind of limbo existence, but also a buffer from the strange new world into which we had moved. It offered us a comfortable transition, but I knew I couldn't just hang out there. I had to figure out what I could do in China. I no longer was director of an international organization, daughter of my parents, sister of my siblings, and friend of my friends. I felt alone, the spouse of a U.S. diplomat, an appendage—"a dependent," in the State Department's (offensive to me) terminology—a rude shock after my years as a professional woman on my own!

Though scared and alone, I knew that if I didn't get out, I would wither. I decided to go across town to visit some people I knew who worked at the China Disabled People's Federation (CDPF). On my previous visit to China representing Very Special Arts and the Kennedy Center, I had worked with their organization and hoped that I would be able to do some work with them now that I was stationed in Beijing. Since we did not have a car yet, I rented a bicycle and set out to cross Beijing through the sea of thousands of bicycles and the maze of *hutongs* (alleys). Entering the vast river of cyclists was terrifying. No one stopped for pedestrians, but neither did they crash into them or each other; all seemed to ebb and flow in a rhythm wholly foreign to me. Westerners, who instinctively seek to go from point A to point B in a direct line, get very frustrated in China, waiting for the bicycles and traffic to stop and let them pass. It doesn't work that way in Beijing; rather, everyone flows like Tai Chi in a constantly moving yin-yang dance.

Shaking from the stress of this first encounter with Beijing, I arrived at the Disabled People's Federation on the far northwest corner of Beijing, feeling triumphant that I had achieved the great feat of navigating Beijing. The people at the Federation were thrilled to see me, but not at all appreciative of what a big deal I found it to have ridden a bicycle there, since they rode bicycles every day.

The Federation was a party-run mass organization directed by Deng Pufang, the son of "paramount leader" Deng Xiaoping. Red Guards had thrown Deng Pufang from a window in the late 1960s during the Cultural Revolution, leaving him paralyzed from the waist down. After his father had regained his power base, Deng Pufang founded the Federation to improve the lives of Chinese disabled people. His position as Deng Xiaoping's son helped bring attention to the issue of disabled people's tribulations and rights. The task was a noble one. Deng Pufang has succeeded in revolutionizing the way Chinese people think about and treat people with disabilities.

Although my old friends were still working at the Federation, it was quickly apparent that it would be impossible for me to work there alongside these Communist party members, even if they did know me. There was no way that a "foreign devil," particularly one married to a U.S. diplomat, would be allowed to actually work at the CDPF, although it was never explained to me in precisely those words. I biked back to the hotel even more discouraged and alone, realizing that I would have to think of other ways to be productive in China.

The colorless post-Mao China of the late 1980s, a very different world from the bustling China of today, heightened my consciousness of being far from home. There were very few cars on the streets and almost none privately owned. Privileged government officials drove around in their long black "Red Flag" limousines. Ordinary government officials and PLA officers were left to drive around in clunky, vintage 1940 motorcycles, toting their wives in sidecars.

By late September, huge towers of white cabbage appeared on every street corner, tucked between houses and lining alleys and sidewalks. With harsh memories of decades of hardship and food shortages, Beijingers bought as much cabbage as they could carry and hauled it home on carts and bicycles to stack, dry, and prepare for the long, harsh north China winter. They would then bury the cabbage around their homes and gradually deplete their hoards through the long freezing winter. In the cabbage season, a remnant from the years of scarcity during the Great Leap Forward and the Cultural Revolution in the 1950s and 1960s, people still felt driven to stockpile white cabbage, even though by 1988 an abundance of vegetables was available in the Beijing markets. Other peculiar habits left from years of fear and repression continue all over China to this day, despite China's increasing modernization. Old habits are hard to break.

In Beijing in 1988, the Chinese government stringently dis- couraged contact between foreigners and Chinese. Foreigners were sequestered in housing compounds reserved for expatriates and off-limits to Chinese. The People's Armed Police guarded the gates to ensure the separation. Jim and I were assigned an apartment in Tayuan, an eight-building high-rise complex situated on the Second Ring Road, about two miles from both the city center and the Embassy. The Tayuan compound was still under construction when we moved in, with cement blocks and dust enveloping our building. We lived on the ninth floor, overlooking the beautiful but odiferous Liangma River, which flowed next to our building toward the Great Wall Hotel. The neighbors on our floor were from Yugoslavia and France.

We were required to use only *waihui* (foreigner's money). The Chinese used *renminbi*, or people's money, though there was a huge black market for *waihui* all over Beijing and other cities. Walking down *hutongs*, one could always hear whispered, "Change money? Change money?" We could only hire housekeepers and Chinese-language teachers through the Chinese government; and they, in turn, had to report on our activities at Saturday afternoon "confession" sessions with their party handlers. However, we somewhat illegally, or extra-legally, hired a cook, Mr. Li, and a housekeeper, Liu Ayi (Auntie Liu), through private connections. Their presence brought a taste of China at its best into our home.

As a first-tour Foreign Service officer, Jim was initially a consular officer, responsible for issuing visas. We quickly learned that virtually every Chinese person wanted to meet us. Despite our hope of making real Chinese friends, most of our Chinese acquaintances eventually requested our help obtaining visas. Each morning, hundreds of people lined up outside of Erban (No. 2 Building) of the American Embassy seeking visas for America. This same scene repeats itself in countries around the world. In each embassy, a consular officer personally interviews each applicant. The consular officer has ultimate authority to issue or deny visas based on that brief interview. Jim denied visas to many people because of the legal presumption that they were immigrants not intending to return to China, unless they could convince him otherwise in the interview. Because of his job, we wondered if we would ever be able to make real Chinese friends.

Chinese people had been taught for decades to distrust "foreign devils," particularly "beautiful imperialists," an epithet for Americans. While language was a real hurdle, so, too, was culture. Americans love the open exchange of ideas and news. Chinese, after decades of living under a closed communist regime, tend to guard what they know, since information is power and provides advantage over neighbors. In the highly confrontational Cultural Revolution, differences were severely punished, in keeping with the old Chinese adage, "The grass blade that sticks up gets cut down." Almost everyone has stories of the terrible repression they faced during the Cultural Revolution. I was afraid that any friend I might make would either distrust me or get into trouble because of my diplomat husband.

The Chinese people had a special name for Consul Jim—*Zuopiezi*, or Lefty—because he was left-handed in a nation of right-handed people. Few of China's billion people had been allowed to use their left hands. Jim and I, oddly enough, are both left-handed. Often at Chinese banquets, we would sit at a great round table of right-handed people. There, Jim and I, using our left hands, would bump elbows with the people next to us, upsetting the symmetry of the table and creating bad *qi* (vibes)—so typical of foreign devils! Our hosts also often had the somewhat annoying courtesy of offering us their most delicious delicacy—huge juicy sea slugs—which we politely tried to eat as they slipped off our chopsticks.

As I walked around the streets of Beijing, I could hear people whispering *"Ta shi zuopiezi de furen"* (she's the wife of lefty). I always wondered whether Jim had denied visas to them, or to their families or friends.

One Saturday morning, Jim was getting a haircut and a shave at a barbershop. The female barber shaving Jim halted the old-fashioned straight-edged razor in the middle of his neck and bore down on the blade saying, "Don't you remember me, Lefty?"

Shakily he said, "I'm not sure, do I know you?"

"Last week, you denied me a visa!" she said pressing the blade against his throat.

In a falsetto voice an octave above normal, he squeaked, "Why don't you come in next week, and I will review your application." She eased up on the razor and proceeded to tell him how vital it was for her to attend a two-week seminar on hair dressing in Los Angeles, after which she would certainly return to China and continue working in the salon. The next week he let his colleagues deny her visa application a second time, and he changed barbershops forever.

The American embassy in Beijing officially designated me a "dependent," a term I found demeaning, reflecting the low status ascribed to spouses in the Foreign Service. The Yiban, or main Embassy chancery building, was inaccessible to me as a spouse without my undergoing the indignity of calling my husband to come down and chaperone me. U.S. embassies offer spouses jobs aptly named PIT (for part-time) positions. These are usually low-paying, often intermittent jobs. None of the positions in Beijing seemed appealing, and I quickly realized that hanging out at the Embassy was not what I wanted to do in China. Embassy Americans spent much of their time complaining about the things they didn't like in China. I wanted to steer clear of that kind of negativism and opted rather to throw myself into the intriguing but challenging world of China, the Middle Kingdom.

China Becomes Real

After declining a low-level position with the U.S. embassy, I looked for and found a Chinese-language tutor. Through him the color and fascination of China started to become real. He was a recent college graduate named Lu Yong. Although the government assigned him to me, Lu Yong taught me Chinese in quite unorthodox ways—taking me around Beijing, going to markets, restaurants, universities, and night clubs. He pointed out the changes occurring in China. Daily we walked the innumerable *hutongs* of Beijing, where we saw young people walking arm in arm, small shops, lovers lying on park benches, diapered babies with slit-crotch pants for convenience, young people in jeans, and even a few girls in miniskirts.

The *hutongs* were lined with dull gray, concrete high-rise apartments that had few windows, public toilets that reeked for blocks, sidewalk noodle shops, and masses of bicyclists moving in unison in an unchoreographed dance. When it rained, bicyclists donned nearly identical rain ponchos, transforming the sea of black bikes into a sea of color. As Lu and I went around Beijing on bicycle, I came to feel that the true rhythm of China was the rhythm of the bicycle—all the same size and color, with the exact same gear sprocket, moving together in unison, their riders chatting about life as they rode along. It was on the bicycle that I became immersed in China, not only colorful and mesmerizing, but constantly moving ahead smoothly, in sync with the bicycle gears.

Early every morning in Ritan (Sun Altar) Park, I practiced Tai Chi, the ancient Chinese art of shadowboxing, with Lu's good friend Zhang Fang. The parks of Beijing still hold onto the magic of traditional China. With their elegant weeping willows, craggy rock gardens set among pagodas and teahouses, and groups of old men meditating or walking and swinging their birdcages, parks carried on the life known in China before communism. Long before dawn each morning, old men gathered in parks, carrying their birdcages so that the birds can sing with each other as the men play music or mah jong. When the sun rises above the trees, they cover the birdcages and take them home. Each morning myriads of older people fill the parks practicing Tai Chi, sword dancing, and even ballroom dancing.

I loved my mornings in the park. As a dancer, I was thrilled to see dancing everywhere I looked. Ironically, while Chinese people all around me were dancing the waltz and tango, I worked at becoming adept at Tai Chi and sword drills. Zhang Fang and I moved in the slow motion of the Tai Chi in cadence with other practitioners around us. It served as a quiet meditation with which I loved to begin my days.

In the evenings, Jim and I often went to Ritan Park to eat *jiaozi* (Chinese dumplings) and drink *sheng pijiu* (Beijing draft beer). The contrast between old and new China was stark. In many ways, people lived just as they had a century ago in the West during the Industrial Revolution—in darkened houses, burning sooty coal for heat and cooking, and struggling to survive. While everyone seemed equal—or, more accurately, equally poor—there was a noticeable, though subtle change, especially among young people, who bore a spark of life, adventure, and hope.

Lu's friends were young and hip. They listened incessantly to rock music from Taiwan. Lu used many of the rock songs as our Chinese "textbook." He taught me the lyrics of the most popular songs, which all the young Chinese knew by heart. At night, we would go to karaoke bars, and I would take my turn on stage singing popular Chinese rock songs. Crowds would throw bouquets of flowers at me in their amazement that a Westerner could follow the bouncing ball on the wall and read Chinese characters.

In fact, I could not read a single Chinese character! In order to focus on learning spoken Chinese, I had opted to skip learning the complex written characters. Lu wrote the characters for me in Pinyin, using Western letters to phonetically spell out words. Then, I would memorize the song lyrics word for word and practice them over and over. I learned to speak current Chinese this way. Although I am sorry today that I can't read Mandarin, it was, for me, a much faster and more enjoyable way to learn Chinese than sitting and memorizing the tens of thousands of characters that make up the language.

The lyrics of many Chinese popular rock songs had double meanings for students in the late 1980s. One of the songs, *"Waimien de Shijie"* ("Outside World"), took on special meaning for PRC students in 1988–89. They knew little about the outside world, since all things Western had been forbidden since 1949. Yet, they were hungry to learn everything about life outside China. This song came to represent their yearning for China to open up and liberalize. When the student movement blossomed in the "Beijing Spring" of 1989, I was able to understand many of the rock music allusions and political double meanings accompanying the huge demonstrations and rallies that electrifying spring. Jim, with his book-learned Chinese, was sometimes clueless.

Chinese society in 1988–89 was still closed and suspicious, and although students were curious about the West, they remained cautious and fearful. Those who knew some English, however, would try to practice. They would walk up to us in parks or on the street and say, "Will you be my friend?" Then they would ask endless questions about the United States. They wanted to know, "Why do you have race problems?" "Why don't you take care of your elders?" "Why are there so many guns and so much crime in your cities?" We would speak slowly and distinctly with them, trying to explain the cultural differences of American society, though their rudimentary English lacked the subtlety needed to discuss these issues in depth.

Lu explained the *danwei* system to me. Chinese life revolved around the *danwei*, the workplace or work unit. All people are members of a *danwei*, which takes care of them. The *danwei* provides jobs, housing, medical care, and often education. At the same time the *danweis* closely control life, telling Chinese people what they could and could not do, even when and how to have sexual relations. The *danwei* got directly involved in the life of married couples, policing how many children were permitted each couple. *Danwei* party leaders sometimes even tracked women's menstrual cycles and restricted births by penalizing salaries and housing options. *Danweis* monitored who one's friends were, with foreign friends particularly dangerous to have, creating a stultifying straitjacket. Basic necessities were provided, yet no one had control over his or her own destiny, perhaps explaining the high level of apathy among many Chinese people I encountered in Beijing. It didn't really matter how hard they worked. There was no way to get ahead of the next guy, neither incentive to give good service nor any urge toward competition. It was hard, if not virtually impossible, to change one's assigned lot in life. Jeffrey, a single man I knew, had to remain living with his parents well into his late thirties and worked in their *danwei*. Apartments went only to married couples.

Living in China reminded me how blessed I was for the freedom I have had, and how fortunate I was to have been born in the United States, especially as a woman. Although the official line in China was that women were equal—"they hold up half the sky," as Mao so glowingly put it—even within the family, old Confucian values lingered and girls did not receive equal treatment. I, on the other hand, had grown up confident that I could do anything I wanted. How ironic, then, that only in the role of Foreign Service spouse did I experience what it means not to have control over my life. I came to appreciate the stamina and courage it takes to break out of these confines. It was my good fortune to meet a number of people during our three years in Beijing who actually did so, as I slowly did as well.

The Ballroom Dance Craze

Eventually, the Chinese Disabled People's Federation (CDPF) decided to use my volunteer services to organize arts workshops in Beijing for disabled people and to teach English to the CDPF staff. They even provided a car and driver each day to take me to schools and workshop locations around Beijing, a huge, far-flung city encompassing great distances.

I visited many institutions for the deaf and blind and orphanages for the mentally handicapped, where I taught adaptive arts techniques to the deaf, blind, and physically disabled, as well as to their teachers. In my previous work as director of Very Special Arts International in Washington, I had worked with more than fifty countries to develop theater troupes with deaf people, dance programs for blind people, dance classes for people in wheel chairs, and visual arts programs for people who had no use of their hands. In China, I shared these skills with the disabled.

Usually the staff and students had never before met a Westerner, much less an American. I surprised them by being different from the propaganda on which they had been raised, and they began calling me "Comrade Joanne." They were cautious but curious. My hope was that they left my classes thinking foreign ways weren't so bad after all! At each school, staff members and disabled students seemed to have a good time learning to create dances, play music, and paint or draw. I was teaching them a whole new way of thinking about the disabled using the arts. I encouraged them to use their imaginations—not a virtue valued in Communist China—and to push their children to do the same. I found my students extremely polite and surprisingly receptive, but wholly unaccustomed to the sense of freedom I sought to cultivate.

In Chinese culture, the arts are done the way the masters have always done them; what Westerners might view as mimicry is considered the highest art form in China. A true artist should replicate the master's brushstroke, reproduce notes in music or voice, or duplicate dance movements just as people have done for thousands of years. Spontaneity and individuality were not encouraged or rewarded in China. Conformity was the model value instilled in a billion Chinese. This was alien to my experience as a dancer and actress in such freewheeling places as Madison, Wisconsin, Berkeley, California, and Cambridge, Massachusetts. When I asked my Chinese students to try something new, to try to move like the wind, like water, or like fire, they looked at me as if I was a bit mad. But they were game and willing to try.

Once I asked a teacher of preschoolers to try walking like an elephant. She turned to me in shocked puzzlement and asked, "Why would anyone want to walk like an elephant?"

"Good question," I responded. "Maybe your students would enjoy the heavy feeling, but only if you show them how first." She laughed and then started to move across the room like a lumbering elephant. Blushing and sheepish, she then ran back to her side of the room and resumed her prim and proper stance.

More often than not, I ended up being the main topic of conversation at the schools and institutions I visited. One memorable day I wore a full body jumpsuit to teach dance to a group of special education teachers. When I asked to use the restroom, the entire group of women escorted me en masse to what turned out to be a large hole in the ground, then stood back and waited. While they conveniently squatted with their skirts swirled modestly about them, I had to take off my entire jump suit and squat down with considerable embarrassment and awkwardness. That day I learned a second lesson—in China, there is no sense of, or need for, privacy as we know it in the West. Our Western need to be alone is strange and alien to Chinese people. I learned, for example, that when you book a massage, hotel staffers walk in and out throughout the exercise, talking nonchalantly with the masseuse. After that day, I began to plan more carefully what I wore.

Around the time we arrived in Beijing, a ballroom dance craze was beginning to sweep the city. Dancing had been forbidden as bourgeois during the Cultural Revolution of the 1960s and 1970s. By the late 1980s, however, people craved to learn Western ballroom dance. One day, two Chinese ballroom dancers came to meet me at my Tai Chi class at the invitation of my martial arts teacher, Zhang Fang. They wanted to see how I danced Latin dances and rock and roll. Amazingly, they weren't at all afraid to dance arm in arm with me right there in Ritan Park. Then they invited me to their studio to give a dance demonstration. All my life, dance has been for me a magical link with people of all ages, cultures, and abilities. So it was in a post-Mao China just waking up to the outside world. Dance, in China as everywhere, transcends language barriers and enables people to communicate nonverbally. I was excited. Perhaps through dance, I could make friends in China.

As my dance reputation spread, I was invited to teach ballroom dance classes in several Beijing schools and universities. In one college, I had over a hundred students eager to learn to waltz, cha cha, tango, fox trot, salsa, meringue, and jitterbug. They loved learning my Western ballroom dances as much as I loved learning their Tai Chi and martial arts. Their infectious enthusiasm bowled me over. It felt odd, even comical, to be introduced as "Comrade Joanne" and then put on "Rock Around the Clock Tonight" and boogie. My hardest task was to get Chinese hips to move like Latin ones—not exactly an easy task, since Chinese people aren't constituted quite the same way, nor accustomed to Latin rhythms.

In 1988, dance was becoming all the rage across Beijing. It was infectious. In every park and public place people were ballroom dancing every morning. Couples, young and old, often very old, could be seen clasping each other tightly, doing the waltz or tango to boom box music at daybreak! Eventually, I was invited to go on Chinese television several times to demonstrate ballroom dance moves with a Chinese partner. For my regular classes, although he was untrained, I drafted Jim into the business, because I needed an obliging partner. Amazingly, Jim and I, although just so-so at square dance, went early each Sunday morning to Jingshan Elementary School to teach the children of Communist Party leaders how to do the very American do-si-do, swing your partner, and promenade. Fred Astaire and Ginger Rogers might have been proud of us, but I don't know about the Gang of Four!

Trying to Get Closer

One evening Jim and I went out with a Chinese couple who were good friends of ours. All four of us rode our black clunker bicycles through the *hutongs* to a bazaar just east of the Forbidden City, where we bought delectable morsels of food at various outdoor food stalls—barbequed quail skewered on bamboo sticks over turning spits, deep fried pork, and rice-flour-with-egg deep fried in oil. We waded through throngs of Beijingers out eating and shopping in the warm evening. We then decided to go dancing at a popular dancing hall. When we arrived, the hall's bouncers wouldn't let Jim and me into this *waiguoren bu neng jin lai* (off-limits to foreigners) establishment, because we were what the party called "flies"—alcohol and cigarette users and polluting foreigners—who would contaminate the people. The party feared Westerners would be a bad influence, bringing sex, drugs, or just bad thoughts. Jim and I and our two friends were greatly disappointed, because we all really wanted to dance that night.

The scars left from the Cultural Revolution, including fear and distrust of foreigners supposedly overruled a decade earlier, were clearly visible everywhere. Almost everyone we met had been affected in some way. After years of repression, Western ideas, people, and influence still intimidated most Chinese people in the late 1980s. The party was trying to hold back the tide of change about to hit China. Little did they know what changes would soon come.

One day, during a visit to Shanghai in late 1988, Jim and I were walking down one of the quaint, tree-lined streets of the old French Concession when we noticed a billboard advertising a motion picture entitled *Aidzibing,* or "Love Sickness" (the Chinese double entendre translation of AIDS). Since my sister Christine and her husband, Anthony Fauci, were deeply involved in AIDS research and prevention at the National Institutes of Health, we decided to see the film to get the Chinese perspective on the disease. It told a story about a young girl who got involved with a Western man — a gangling, big-nosed, loud-mouthed, loose, sleazy kind of guy, who drank large quantities of hard liquor, listened to raucous jazz, and smoked huge cigars. The beautiful, sweet, innocent Chinese girl eventually became sick after spending time with him. She tested positive for the then-strange disease *Aidzibing.* Then the real disaster struck: She became an outcast, shunned by family and friends and locked up in a cold gray institution. She grew ghastly ill and lost her mental faculties. All fingers pointed to the corrupt and deceitful Westerner. The clear moral of the film was: stay away from nasty, dirty, disease-laden Westerners and you won't get AIDS.

When the lights came up at the end of the film, we realized to our — and the audience's — horror that we were the only Westerners in the theater. When we exited the theater, it was like the parting of the Red Sea, as people scurried to avoid us. This was the extent of AIDS education in the PRC in the late 1980s, long before the government was willing to admit how prevalent AIDS had become in China. Disturbed, I wrote a letter to my sister and Tony to encourage some constructive dialogue and medical exchanges with China. Tony actually did a WorldNet broadcast to hundreds of Chinese doctors, who asked him many questions about medical protocols for AIDS patients. I even ended up speaking on several panels to promote AIDS education. In 1988 and 1989, China clearly had a long way to go before even beginning to deal with its incipient AIDS epidemic.

Under the auspices of the CDPF, the China Disabled People's Federation, I started visiting and working at Qinghe Orphanage, a concrete gray institution on the banks of the Qing Canal in the Northern outskirts of Beijing. It was a large orphanage, with over 750 children, many disabled. Most had only minor problems, such as a cleft palette, but an inordinate number of the orphans were girls. Being female, it seems, was still one of the greatest "disabilities" in Communist China. Since China permitted each couple only one child, the preferred child was almost invariably male. Girl babies were often abandoned whether or not they had any disability.

Much to my dismay, the children in the orphanage were confined to their beds all day long, atrophying in mind and body. There were few toys, and no activities other than eating and sleeping. I urged the staff to get the children out of bed and let me work with them. They were surprised but complied. Together, step by step, we slowly began to try new things with the kids—like music and movement, drawing and singing. The children soaked up the activities like sponges. The work was bittersweet, though, as they would cling to me when I had to leave, not wanting me to go. This need overwhelmed me.

To address the tremendous need in the Qinghe Orphanage, I decided to organize Beijing International Volunteers—BIV for short. Many people in the international community wanted to get involved with the local Chinese community but didn't know how. When I offered a training course on adaptive arts and disability, forty people volunteered to help out and were trained alongside the orphanage staff. I explained how to teach music, dance, theater, and visual arts to deaf, blind, and physically and mentally disabled people. After six weeks of training, these volunteers began working once a week with children in the orphanage. We soon had a steady stream of foreigners coming and going every working hour of every day, teaching arts, drama, music, sports, and games to the children. Life and laughter came to this once cold, forlorn place. The children in the orphanage came alive. They would beg the volunteers not to leave at the end of their sessions with them, clinging to them and rushing to block the door. The unusual mixing of Westerners and Chinese was stimulating for adults and children alike and the Qinghe Orphanage began to change.

CDPF Federation director Deng Pufang expressed appreciation for the work we were doing. With his approval, our work was able to continue at Qinghe. BIV organized several clothing and toy drives for the children, who had almost no toys. After making each presentation, however, I would return a few days later, and to my dismay, find the toys locked up in a closet far removed from the children. The staff would explain that "the children fight over the toys, so we had to lock them up." To circumvent this obstacle, I purchased 750 identical black and white stuffed panda bears, and personally put one in each child's bed. Thinking I had solved the problem, I was pleased to know that each child now had a toy all his or her own and no one would feel left out.

One day, however, when I showed up unexpectedly at the orphanage, there were no stuffed bears to be seen. They had once again vanished. I couldn't believe it! I walked angrily down the hall, only to discover to my amazement a workshop where staff members were making stuffed panda bears exactly like the ones BIV had donated. The orphanage directors had created a small factory making panda bears for profit and had sold the ones I'd donated. Although they were indeed resourceful, I felt they had betrayed the children and me.

In Chinese culture, copying an idea or great work of art is perfectly acceptable. Copyrights and intellectual property rights are new and quite alien to China. Replicating a good idea is not considered stealing, merely laudable imitation of the masters and the highest form of flattery. For example, Jim and I had befriended a fine artist, Liu Yongli, who produced beautiful oil paintings of Chinese scenes—creatively marrying Western technique with traditional Chinese motifs. We visited his studio on numerous occasions and eventually bought two of his best pieces at prices closer to American than 1980s Chinese. We were thrilled with our unique new paintings and proudly hung them in our living room. One night, however, we decided to drop in on him at his studio unannounced. Entering his loft, we found him making replicas of *our* painting! We were astonished! "How can you do this, copy an original piece of art? This is dishonest!" we protested. He apologized profusely and said that he was only painting it for his brother and would never sell it. We departed, less than reassured and fearing that our painting would end up on every foreigner's wall in Beijing. Such is the clash between the traditional Chinese practice of copying the masters and the Western belief in the sacred uniqueness of each work of art.

Jim and I frequently took trips outside of Beijing. We visited the famous beach at Beidaihe, the seaside resort north of Tianjin kept for the almost exclusive use of Communist leaders. We traveled to the holy mountain of Taishan and climbed its thousands of stairs to "Heaven," ploddingly lifting our feet step by step until our legs felt like jelly, while Buddhist monks and coolies, stripped to the waist, literally ran up and down the endless staircase next to us, carrying heavy loads on poles balanced on their shoulders. We went to the beautiful Qing Imperial Summer Palace in Yiheyuan in the middle of winter and marveled at the elegance of the palaces covered in a white blanket of snow. We had many picnics at the regal Ming Tombs and the nearby magnificent Great Wall, north of Beijing. Each trip brought us closer to Chinese history and traditions. The Chinese countryside is a world away from Beijing, much quainter, simpler, and less affected by the Communist overlay that characterized Beijing.

I especially liked Shanghai, a huge metropolis, but one with a more human scale and a much milder climate than Beijing. The CDPF sent me down to Shanghai for a week to train special educators in adaptive arts techniques. I had a wonderful time exploring the small alleyways of old Shanghai, full of colorful people, food, music, and life. I especially loved the old Willow Tea House situated on an island in a lake in the heart of the old section. Reached by crossing the zigzagged bridge that blocked evil spirits, who only travel in straight lines, there I would eat a large bowl of noodles, drink steaming pots of fragrant tea from nearby Hangzhou, and listen to the playing of a two stringed *erhou*. I loved to chat with the old Chinese men who played mah jong and sang folk songs. It was a fascinating place with an ancient China flair, in the heart of that great city built by foreigners.

Jim had written his dissertation on the fabled foreign concessions of old Shanghai, and we had fun exploring the former International Settlement and French Concession. The Shanghai we visited in the late 1980s was frozen in time, with few changes from the pre-1949 city. The old Peace Hotel, towering over the Bund along the Whangpoo River, retained the color and feel of the 1940s. Its lobby still had a dark little bar featuring a jazz band that had been playing there since those days. There was little indication in this crumbling time capsule of the profound changes that would come to China and to Shanghai beginning in the mid 1990s.

Walking down the old streets of the International Settlement, Jim and I found the old American Club, the Shanghai American School, and Gracie Gale's Bawdyhouse, which had been run by a corseted American woman with a throaty voice like Tallulah Bankhead's. The once-elegant old foreign mansions had been subdivided into worker apartments, party headquarters, and cooperatives. They were but pale reflections of their former glory. Though rundown, the elegant colonial style of the neighborhoods was still visible, and you could imagine the extraordinarily privileged life of old Shanghai, a life reserved for the foreigner. Jim's research had traced this colonialist society, which served as breeding grounds for the Communist Revolution in China and spawned the deep distrust of foreigners that ensued for decades. How ironic that Shanghai today is again swarming with foreigners!

Changes in the Air, Tiananmen Square

In the spring of 1989, Jim and I were swept up by the events of "Beijing Spring," the student democracy movement. On April 15, Hu Yaobang, the popular but disgraced former Communist Party general secretary who had been banished because of his liberal views, suddenly died. In the days that followed, hundreds, then thousands of students at Beijing University (Beida) and other universities and colleges began calling for recognition of Hu Yaobang, which gradually turned into a call for greater democracy.

Jim's major professor from the University of North Carolina, Michael Hunt, was then doing research for a book at Beijing University. Three days after Hu's death, we went with him to see a film on campus about the Korean War from the Chinese point of view. I was shocked to see how Americans were portrayed as the bad guys attacking the brave, selfless Chinese soldiers, the very reverse of all that I had learned about the Korean War growing up in America. When we came out of the campus movie theater, we found students milling about "the Triangle," reading slogans tacked to the walls and holding impromptu discussions unprecedented in Communist China. We mingled among the students and listened to some of their ideas. Seeing us, they thanked us for coming, saying "*Meiguo hen hao*" (America is good) and asked us how students in the United States demonstrated and about our student days during the Vietnam War era. A large crowd gathered around us as we tried to discuss our experiences demonstrating against the Vietnam War in the United States.

Over the next week we watched the movement grow, each day expecting the government to crack down. On May 4, the sacred anniversary of the 1919 May 4th Student movement, students poured out of university campuses into the streets. The numbers increased each day, first hundreds, then thousands of students marching around the second ring road encircling Beijing, calling for freedom, for the right to be heard, and for dialogue with party leaders. Amazingly, the government leaders did not respond but stayed secluded in their privileged refuge of Zhongnanhai adjacent to the Forbidden City and Tiananmen Square. A Beijing Normal University student named Chai Ling made an emotional plea for the government to engage in talks with the students; otherwise they were going to stage a hunger strike to demand direct negotiations with party leaders. When no response was forthcoming from Zhongnanhai, the students descended by the thousands on Tiananmen Square, set up camp at the foot of Mao Zedong's mausoleum, and launched the hunger strike on May 13. Mao must have been turning over in his grave! Although he knew all too well the power of mobilized students driven by nationalistic fervor, as the Red Guards had been during the Cultural Revolution, he would have been horrified to think that students would actually call for democracy and freedom *from* the Communist party!

Meanwhile, Lu Yong continued my Chinese lessons. With the streets full of people, we had so much to discuss. Most of what was happening in Beijing that spring was a new phenomenon for Lu. We had animated conversations trying to predict where all this was leading. My vocabulary was full of new Chinese words that had not been spoken in China in decades—words like democracy, freedom, demonstration, protest. The air was electric. Over the next week, the square filled with colorful banners, loudspeakers blaring, and hundreds of tents with thousands of people. It was an amazing event to be living through! In mid-May, Soviet Premier Mikhail Gorbachev arrived in Beijing on an official visit. The first Russian head of state to visit China in thirty years, Gorbachev arrived at the Great Hall of the People for his historic meeting with Deng Xiaoping. The entire international press corps came to Beijing to cover the momentous meeting between the Chinese and the Soviets. Much to the embarrassment of the Chinese government, however, what they ended up covering was the student movement and occupation of Tiananmen Square, which turned out to be a far more interesting story.

ABC, CBS, NBC, CNN, BBC, and international press from all over the world set up cameras in Tiananmen Square awaiting Gorbachev's arrival and, in the meantime, focused on the fasting students. The night before the Gorbachev visit, students confronted police on the steps of the Great Hall of the People, which runs along the Western side of Tiananmen Square. Because the media was at the ready and captured the drama, the entire world was drawn into the student movement. The video images of Chinese students broadcast worldwide aroused international sympathy for their struggle.

Busy and emboldened by the worldwide attention and support, students continued streaming into the square. People arrived from the countryside by the train carload and poured into Beijing, turning Tiananmen Square into a people's camp. It was memorable for Jim and me to witness this thawing and awakening of the people of China. The air was electric with the excitement of debate, criticism, and new ideas. Students were speaking publicly and testing their skills with new political slogans. Each day, Jim and I wandered through throngs of students on street corners and in parks, deep in heretofore-prohibited political debate. We watched them grow bolder by the day and increasingly vocal and sure of their ideas. We saw average Beijingers wake up from the years of intellectual slumber and oppression and begin to smile and express a sense of hope. The movement spread from street corner to street corner, to offices, shops, and worker cooperatives. We would stand discreetly on the margins and listen to the conversations. We could almost feel the opening up of people's hearts and minds, like watching a dead flower come back to life. It was an astounding experience. Students, workers, old and young people, shopkeepers, even Communist Party members—people who had been numb for years—all began smiling, greeting each other, speaking out in public, and defending their rights in the street. By the end of May, tens of thousands of permanent demonstrators occupied Tiananmen Square.

After a while, the student hunger strike began to lose force. Medical supplies flowed in from Hong Kong. Students on cots in hospital tents lay in the square with IV's in their arms. Medics rushed in and out of the square offering first aid. Order began to deteriorate, as garbage grew in mountains all over the square. The students established volunteer brigades to direct traffic, transport food and medical supplies, and patrol the streets and *hutongs*. It was amazing and unprecedented in Maoist China—the students and their supporters were effectively in control of large swaths of Beijing, as police and soldiers stayed out of sight and Beijing's leaders hovered deep inside Zhongnanhai. The students proclaimed they were setting up "a real people's government."

Meanwhile, Communist Party leaders seemed hesitant and confused. They did not respond to calls for dialogue; there appeared to be no leadership. Finally, on May 19, Premier Zhao Ziyang, the most liberal-minded person in the ruling Politburo, went out to meet with the students in the square. With tears in his eyes, he pleaded with them to stop their hunger strike and leave. We later learned that he knew what was about to happen. Late on May 30, Vice Premier Li Peng went on television surrounded by members of the Politburo, stiffly dressed in Mao suits. He soberly announced that the government was sending troops in to restore order. By this time, Premier Zhao Ziyang had disappeared from sight, ousted for disagreeing with the hard-liners' decision to move in on the students. Zhao was placed under house arrest and was never seen in public again. Many years later, however, his memoir was released posthumously and published. In it he described the events inside the leadership during that trying time for the Communist party.

On the night of June 1, Jim went to Tiananmen Square at around 7 p.m. as he had done each evening. He watched as young, unarmed PLA troops tried to reach the square only to be turned back by the students and workers, who convinced the soldiers not to hurt their fellow Beijingren. Before midnight, joyful celebrations rippled through the square as the students realized they had actually stopped the army from entering the city!

The next morning, the government announced martial law and clamped down on all media. With the entire world watching, broadcasters were shut down, some right in mid-sentence. Tom Brokaw was pushed off the set while broadcasting, and the screen went black as millions of people in America watched. International reporters were physically and visibly forced to leave the square. The airwaves from China to the rest of the world went black.

Nevertheless, on June 2, thousands of people ignored martial law and rode their bicycles to Tiananmen Square in support of the students. Jim and I, too, solemnly biked with them through the streets and around the square. We could sense a strange mixture of exhilaration and foreboding, as no one was certain what would happen next. No police were even visible. The students seemed to be running the city—directing traffic and maintaining order. They set up checkpoints at all of the entrances to the city. I continued to drive our ancient Toyota, which with its diplomatic license plates plowed through the sea of demonstrators, who parted like the Red Sea. Giving me the V-for-victory sign, they would shout "Lao Wai" (honorable outsider) and wave me through.

After foreign media broadcasts were cut off, it became difficult to find out what was happening. The government began broadcasting over loudspeakers in the square and on street corners, with heavy surrealistic propaganda proclaiming, "The army loves the people, and the people love the army." The airwaves were filled with PLA martial choruses singing patriotic marching songs and pledging to restore peace. On television, PLA soldiers, caked in makeup, danced in flowing white chiffon capes to marching music. The only way to know what was really happening, however, was to make the long trek down to Tiananmen Square and watch. Jim and I went each evening that week.

In the middle of all this turbulence and uncertainty, Jim's sixty-seven-year-old mother, Helen Morris, arrived from Alabama for a visit. We took her to visit the square, where she talked with students and inescapably got swept up in the events with us. She went to see the twenty-one-foot alabaster white statue, modeled after the Statue of Liberty, that the students had erected in the middle of the square and named the "Goddess of Democracy." Helen snapped photographs of the statue and all that she witnessed in the square. Although the students occupied Tiananmen and were camped out at the entrance to Zhongnanhai, where the party leaders lived, the leadership maintained an eerie quiet.

On the evening of June 2, another brigade of PLA troops,

this time from remote villages, nearly succeeded in reaching the square. Several thousand young men, appearing no older than fifteen years, marched west along Jianguomen Boulevard toward the square. The people surrounded them, however, and convinced them not to attack. The young boy soldiers were dazed and scared, holding hands like children on a playground. Sent in fresh from the countryside, they had no idea what they were getting into. Their trucks were surrounded by swarms of demonstrators, who smothered them in kindness and tried to educate them about the events in Beijing and urge them to join in. Jim, Helen, and I walked among the dialoguing groups as victory again reverberated across the square. Celebrations went on until the early morning hours of June 3rd.

The evening of June 3 seemed to be a repeat of the preceding nights. Helen, Jim and I spent the early evening walking around the square talking to the students. Helen and I said goodnight to Jim around 9:30 p.m. and took a cab back to our apartment on the second ring road, leaving Jim behind in the square. On our way home, we stopped at the Great Wall Hotel, where we sensed a lot of anxiety among the press gathered there. Many thought some kind of confrontation was inevitable, otherwise the government would just cease to exist. We then returned to our apartment. At about ten in the evening, just before Helen went to bed, Jim called and told me to come back to the square.

Before she slept, Helen said, "This day has been amazing, the students have such zeal. The democracy movement seems so strong that the government can't stop them."

"I know," I said, "It is unbelievable that the students could turn back the army night after night. What a remarkable thing to live through!" I kissed her goodnight and decided to go back to the square to meet Jim and join them celebrating in Tiananmen Square once again.

I jumped into a cab and tried to get back into the square, but this time people surrounded my cab and told me to go back and leave. People sensed danger. With fear in their eyes, they anxiously shouted, "Go home, quickly, you can't go through. It is not safe!" I went home and waited on pins and needles.

Once I returned to my apartment, I heard a rising roar in the streets below and the apartments began to shake a bit. My heart sank. I looked out and saw a seemingly endless column of tanks rolling swiftly towards the city center. Knowing that Jim was in Tiananmen Square, I frantically called the embassy.

"Do you know where Jim Huskey is? Have you heard from him?" I asked the Marine guard on duty.

"Sorry Madame, we have no contact," he responded. "Things are a bit confusing right now."

For the next few hours, no one at the Embassy knew Jim's whereabouts.

As it turned out, Jim was one of the key embassy officers to witness firsthand the nightlong massacre at Tiananmen. When the shooting started as the tanks advanced toward Tiananmen Square from the West along Changan Boulevard, students and workers ran westward from Tiananmen to meet the long column of soldiers and tanks, and Jim ran with them. Everyone assumed the bullets were rubber until people started falling to the pavement in pools of blood. One little old lady ran toward the advancing soldiers and tanks crying, "*Zhonguo ren bu neng sha Zhonguo ren*" (Chinese cannot kill Chinese). A man standing next to Jim was hit in the middle of his forehead. Jim ducked behind trees in front of the Gate of Heavenly Peace of the Forbidden City, then retreated eastward along Jianguomen Boulevard, the Avenue of Eternal Peace, watching as people were machine-gunned by their own government. He saw people run out in front of the tanks and stand in protest. He and a CNN cameraman saw one armored personnel carrier set on fire, a PLA soldier dragged from it and beaten to death by the angry crowds. Jim spent the night watching wave after wave of PLA machine guns mow down protesters all around the area. From midnight to dawn, he ran on and off Jianguomen Boulevard following each round of shooting to count the wounded and the dead.

After a night of counting bodies and helping Americans and others get out of the area, Jim ended up exhausted at the Beijing Hotel in the early morning in the embassy's 17th floor room overlooking the destruction on Jianguomen Boulevard and Tiananmen Square. He returned to the Embassy midmorning on June 4. In a fury of emotion, he wrote a long descriptive cable to the State Department outlining minute by minute what he had seen on the night of June 3–4, the night the Chinese government killed its own people. His key eyewitness report detailed the events of the night.

A few days later, Ambassador Lilley sent a letter to President George H. W. Bush calling Jim "a hero among men" for helping to get people to safety that night. When the Chinese government later tried to deny that anyone was killed in the square that night, Jim's account was one piece of evidence that reported the truth of what actually happened in Tiananmen Square.

He made his way home late on June 5, utterly shaken by what he had witnessed. At last, relief and joy at seeing him safe replaced my anxiety.

Evacuation

In the chaotic days that followed, I joined other embassy members in manning the phones at the Embassy, calling all Americans in the Beijing consular district who had registered with the embassy and answering questions from Americans calling in from across China. Many were panicked and didn't know if they should stay where they were or leave China. Thousands of people thronged the Beijing airport trying to leave.

On June 5, I decided to take Jim's mother to the airport to try to get her out of China. With thousands of desperate foreigners crowding the terminal at the airport, there seemed no hope that she would find a seat. After hours of waiting in unmoving lines, and with the chutzpah and ingenuity that one develops living in the Third World, I walked around the long lines of people waiting at the chaotic ticket counters, entered through the back door of the ticket office, grabbed an official seal, and stamped Helen's ticket to verify the date change. As government clerks protested in Chinese, "*Ni bu Keyi*" (You can't do that), I ran out with the altered and stamped ticket, replying in English, "I don't understand Chinese" (although I understood every word) and pushed Helen through lines and lines of people and right onto a plane. After thirty-six hours, when she arrived back in Dothan, Alabama, she was a local heroine, appearing on television and in the local press describing and showing photos of her ordeal in tumultuous China.

In Beijing a few days later, as the security situation continued to deteriorate, Ambassador Lilley called a meeting of all embassy families and told us that he was ordering a "voluntary evacuation." While he was speaking, however, a barrage of gunfire broke out in front of the Embassy and the ambassador changed his order on the spot to mandatory evacuation of all nonessential personnel. He gave us an hour to prepare to leave China. Anxious and upset by the sudden turn of events, I wanted to say good-bye to Jim, who was out convoying American students and tourists from their university campuses and hotels in northwestern Beijing toward the airport on the east side of the city. Nervously, I waited at the Embassy for him to return. As I waited, Chinese troops opened fire again, this time on the nearby diplomatic high-rise apartments on Jianguomenwai Street. Someone shoved a phone in my hand and said, "Help them!" I started talking with embassy families over the telephone as the soldiers were shooting up their apartments. I urged them to run for the U.S. Marine van waiting outside the compound. "Leave your things behind. Just go quickly!" I told them. The family of the regional security officer was literally under their beds talking to me on the phone while bullets bounced off the walls in their apartment. They eventually made it to safety. Luckily no American was hurt during the attack. Senseless violence and anarchy seemed to prevail in the streets of Beijing.

Along with all the other embassy families and nonessential personnel, I was evacuated and transported to wait for the night at the Lido Hotel on the airport road. The evacuees had brought the oddest assortment of things. What do you take with you when you have a half hour to pack and don't know if you will ever return? Foreign Service families have faced similar evacuations again and again in countries around the world. Some people grabbed their children from school, others their dogs, sterling silverware, or important papers. Luckily, we did not have any children then to worry about.

Preparing to leave, I was alone, since Jim was still out ferrying Americans to safety. I wasn't sure I would even get to see him before I left China the next morning. I also didn't know if I would ever come back to China. With foreboding in my heart that night of June 8, I had closed the door to our apartment in Beijing, leaving everything behind, including my husband, and gone hastily with the Marines to the Lido Hotel to await evacuation.

In the middle of the night, however, there was a knock at the door of my room. Miraculously, it was Jim. He had taken the risk of slipping past unfriendly PLA barricades that had sprung up all over the city and driven out to the Lido Hotel, where we were all awaiting evacuation the next morning. Our embrace was one of immense relief. He collapsed in bed, worn out from driving embassy vans through roadblocks of hostile PLA soldiers. At least we had the night to say good-bye, but how long the separation would be we did not know. How many other Foreign Service couples have had to live through this kind of uncertainty!

The next morning, I was evacuated from China amid the continuing chaos at the Beijing airport. There was a huge sense of relief as embassy families boarded the chartered United Airlines passenger jet. Everyone had been surprisingly calm until one child fell and skinned his knee, and his crying started us all crying. When a United flight attendant said to us, "You can relax now, we are taking you home," we were immensely relieved to be leaving the chaos of Beijing on an American plane with an American crew going to the USA! We finally felt safe after weeks of confusion.

Landing in Tokyo was like coming out of a vacuum. We had been in the center of the maelstrom; but with all media blocked, we had been cut off from the international uproar it had generated. At the airport in Tokyo, news people shoved cameras in our faces, bombarding us with demands for interviews. CBS News asked me to do an interview right there on the spot, but our plane was departing for San Francisco, and I ran for the gate.

By the time I arrived in San Francisco, CBS was waiting for me and again pleaded with me to go on television. Other evacuees were reluctant to speak to the media out of fear for the safety of their spouses still in China. Since my last name, Grady, was different from Jim's, I felt I could do the interview and tell the story with some anonymity for Jim back in Beijing.

CBS put me up in a San Francisco hotel. After days of evacuation in grubby clothes, I ran to a nearby shop and bought a dress to wear for the CBS News interview. That night, immediately following President George H. W. Bush's live address to the nation about the events in China, Dan Rather interviewed me about the Tiananmen massacre. I related all that had happened to us, how the Chinese people of Beijing had been so welcoming to Americans, and how we'd been called *Lao Wai* (foreign friends) during the two-month democracy movement. I described the anarchy of unruly soldiers shooting at random and our hurried exit en masse. As I stepped out of the studio, I saw footage of Tiananmen rolling on the wall bank of television monitors. Seeing for the first time what I had just lived through, I broke down in tears. My father in New Jersey called me and said, "Sweetie, how are you? We saw you on television, but your hair was a mess and you looked so tired! Are you OK?"

"Daddy," I cried, "if you only knew what I have just gone through."

But, how could he, how could anyone viewing China through a television camera, comprehend the enormity of what had happened? China suddenly felt like a world apart.

Meanwhile, Jim remained in Beijing as part of the embassy's skeletal crew working long, isolated hours. They lived and worked in a hostile environment with machine gun–toting troops surrounding the Embassy. He had left our car (with its very visible diplomatic license plates) parked right in Tiananmen Square directly in front of the Great Hall of the People on the night of the massacre. There it sat between PLA tanks guarding the square. Ten days after the massacre, Jim timidly returned to the square to try to retrieve the old Toyota. He walked alone across the vast empty square, through a column of tanks, past a long line of PLA soldiers standing guard and ringing the square. Then, with thousands of eyes following his every step, he used his key to open the car door and, with pretended nonchalance, drove the car back across the square past hundreds of soldiers and out of the square.

During my evacuation in the United States, I was separated from Jim for four months. While staying with my sister Christine in Washington, I faced another facet of diplomacy—explaining the world to Americans. With U.S. attention riveted on China, church groups and community organizations asked me to speak about what was happening inside China. People were both curious and supportive. Having experienced China's ebullient "Beijing Spring" and then its totalitarian crackdown had made me appreciate anew American democracy and the freedom to which I had been born.

Evacuation is an awkward existence and one that Foreign Service families have had to deal with over the years. Evacuees are homeless, jobless, and left hanging for months of total uncertainty. Some have nowhere to go. I lived a peripatetic life in limbo for more than three months, visiting family members and friends and staying with my sister. They hosted many parties and gatherings and dinners to welcome me home; all were anxious to hear about the events in China. Telling Americans about everything that had happened became my purpose during these months.

We were finally allowed to return "home" to China in October 1989. It felt as though I were going through a long tunnel that deposited me a hundred years earlier in a strange land. I returned with a number of other spouses, and Jim was waiting for me at the foot of the ramp with flowers and open arms. Our ambassador, James Lilley, was there waving an American flag, along with the media and a battery of cameras and microphones. We were all overjoyed to be reunited.

The harsh crackdown had left everyone, foreigners and Chinese alike, jittery. Our Chinese friends were afraid to fraternize openly with us. It was too dangerous for them. The differences in China were stark. The government had reverted to heavy propaganda and ideological controls over the people. Ironically, while Eastern Europe was going through a huge turmoil, with each nation, one by one, liberating itself from years of Communist oppression, China clamped down on its people. The Chinese people had no access to the information about Eastern Europe but, rather, were once again experiencing the heavy hand of "big brother." We feared our phones were tapped. We were sometimes followed when we left the diplomatic compound. Our Chinese friends were visited by the security police and harassed for meeting with us. One friend of mine from a deaf school, for which I did some fundraising, was arrested after I met with him one day in a park to give him a donation. It was a different world from the one before Tiananmen, one that the Chinese people understood all too well, but one in which Jim and I had to learn to live.

Made in China

After I returned to Beijing, we made up for lost time, taking advantage of the cessation of virtually all social activities to spend time together at home, and lo and behold, I became pregnant! This would be our evacuation baby! Jim was thrilled beyond belief with the news. In fact, he didn't really believe it until he saw the miniscule curlicue of a fetus on the ultrasound screen at Peking Hospital.

It was fun being pregnant in China. The Chinese adore children. Chinese women lectured me on what I should and shouldn't do according to traditional Chinese lore to remain healthy. I should not wear skirts because the baby would get "wind," which was bad for some reason. I should eat lots of walnuts to develop the baby's brain (hmm, walnuts do look like brains!). I should not exercise too much, should stop doing Tai Chi, and should stay at home. I did not take all of the advice to heart, however, for I continued teaching ballroom dance far into my pregnancy, even teaching the risqué Lambada at seven months pregnant. Lambada is an intimate, sexy dance, but oddly enough the men I danced with never once asked about the solid protuberance at my waist, and I never mentioned it.

To my great delight, the American embassy medical unit sent me to Hong Kong for my obstetric checkups. What a treat! Coming from surrealistic post-massacre Beijing, going to Hong Kong was like being a kid in a candy store. Hong Kong is modern, vibrant, exciting, and worldly. I delighted in staying in a full-service hotel, shopping, drinking high tea at the Mandarin Oriental, and enjoying the luxuries that Hong Kong offered. When I called Jim, I told him I had died and gone to a heaven called Hong Kong!

By contrast, life in Beijing after June 4 was particularly sad and harsh. Americans were viewed as the enemy, at least by the party and government. We represented a "virus" that the Chinese government was trying to wipe out. To use one of Deng Xiaoping's well-known analogies, we were the flies they wanted to keep out when they opened the window (to the West). America stood for democracy, a word now spoken in hushed tones, if at all, in China. The government's anti-American propaganda was heavy and reminiscent of Maoist China. The television was swarming with singing and dancing PLA soldier demonstrations straight from the theater of the absurd. All the while, pubescent soldiers with AK-47s surrounded the American Embassy.

At Halloween, the embassy threw a big party to help break the months of heaviness. Members of the American community, hungry for an enjoyable evening, came costumed as ghosts, mummies, and Draculas. Several turned up dressed as student demonstrators and even gun-toting PLA soldiers! The young Chinese soldiers on guard at the Embassy that evening were puzzled and suspicious that Chinese democracy dissidents might slip past them disguised in Halloween costumes. The guards confronted each arriving costumed guest with their machine guns poised, demanding the masquerader to remove his or her mask. I may have gone a bit far by dressing in a long white robe as the "Goddess of Democracy," who had so recently reigned over Tiananmen Square. I felt nervous, but a little proud, holding my Goddess of Democracy torch as the guards frisked me.

In the ensuing weeks, relations remained tense between our two nations. The Chinese government was enraged because the U.S. Embassy was housing a prime democracy leader, Professor Fang Lizhi, who had fled there for safety on the morning of June 4. On orders from Washington, Ambassador Lilley let him into the Embassy and offered him asylum. He remained almost a year in the ambassador's compound, which was surrounded and heavily guarded by armed PLA soldiers night and day. The tense relations between our nation and China filled the air.

Holding Up Half the Sky

During this tense time, Ambassador Lilley encouraged me to maintain my low-key contacts with Chinese people. Since I had worked directly with Deng Xiaoping's son's organization and with numerous other Chinese people, he asked me to keep him abreast of any news, changes, or insights I might pick up. I thus served as an "unofficial" diplomat with ties to Chinese people, at a time when most official ties were severed.

My Beijing International Volunteer project withered under the intense political crackdown and by late autumn 1989 had become reduced to me alone. I continued, however, to visit orphanages by myself. My friends at the Disabled People's Federation were prohibited from associating with foreigners. Cut off from freely working with disabled people, I began looking around for new opportunities. I wrote to contacts in the United States, offering to serve as a business broker in China.

In early 1990, an American women's group asked me to help organize a U.S.-China Women's Conference. I approached the China Women's Federation, another mass party organization, and broached the proposal. As it happened, they were then bidding to host the 1995 UN Conference on Women and saw a U.S.-China conference as an opportunity to practice organizing an international women's conference. Even though official relations between our two countries were at rock bottom, the Chinese Women's Federation decided to proceed with the conference! Since this would be the first U.S.-China conference since the Tiananmen massacre, both sides proceeded with great caution.

As liaison between the American delegation and the Chinese hosts, I worked with both sides on the substance of papers, organization of events, and topics for dialogue. It was a challenging but wonderful project to have as my pregnancy progressed. Each day I would meet with the women's committee to develop the conference program. The women on the committee were clearly under pressure from their superiors to tow the party line. They had been given authority to invite representatives to the conference from each of the provinces of China and to decide what topics they would be allowed to discuss. I found the censorship offensive and frustrating, particularly as an American used to the free flow of ideas and opinions. I met with many Chinese women to discuss issues that affect women in China and worked with them to develop the themes that should be raised in the conference. Unfortunately, when I went to meet these women, Chinese security police often tailed me. After I had left a group of people, the police would go in and tell the women not to talk to me again, because I was a *weixian fenzi* (dangerous element). My women friends would tell me about these visits when they called me using code names. One friend whose name was Sun, identified herself as "Sunny" on the phone. Another named Wei was just "W" on the phone. They wanted to talk and continued to contact me, despite the harassment they received.

One Chinese woman I met during this rough period was a young artist. She was most unusual in that she was living unmarried with a man in one of the subdivided traditional courtyard houses on an ancient *hutong* in east Beijing. The couple was open and quite colorful and often invited Jim and me to tea to talk about life, politics, and art. I loved to go there, surrounded by paintings and the smell of oil and acrylic, for relaxed and stimulating conversation far from any communist party oversight. We would spend hours drinking tea in the late afternoon, while all the while my baby grew inside me.

When the formal Women's Conference opened in Beijing in June 1990, one year after Tiananmen, the Chinese participants were not allowed to say anything negative about the life of women in China. The official line dominated all Chinese presentations: life for a Chinese woman was totally satisfying and "harmonious." They had no problems with husbands, health, violence, or depression. All was socialist bliss. The American women at the conference, however, poured out their experiences with date rape, stress, divorce, single parenthood, and other challenges facing women in the United States. It was glaringly imbalanced and made me feel uncomfortable and extremely discouraged after all the planning and organizing.

We called the conference "Holding Up Half the Sky," from the old Maoist saying. Despite the Chinese government's attempt to control all dialogue at the conference, there was much that was useful, even stimulating, on the margins of the conference. In the hallways and in private meetings, women did what they always do—talked, formed friendships, and supported each other. This conference, with women from two countries and two worlds meeting and discussing issues, was exhilarating, even under the post-Tiananmen restrictions.

On the opening day of the women's conference, dissident Fang Lizhi, who had taken refuge inside the U.S. embassy for almost a year, was secretly allowed to depart China and go to the United States. Unknown to us, as Ambassador Lilley's wife, Sally, was making the opening remarks at our U.S.-China Women's Conference, Fang was being quietly spirited to the airport and to freedom, under a secret arrangement between our two governments. As we were opening up dialogue between Chinese and American women, relations between our two governments remained extremely tense and suspicious.

By the end of the women's conference, the baby inside me was kicking restlessly. With the conference over, I was finally able to leave. At thirty-six weeks pregnant I flew for twenty hours to the United States to have my baby. Since it was far beyond the airline's seven-month recommended limit, I tried to look as unpregnant as I could by camouflaging my body under a big flowing dress. Marissa, the four-year-old daughter of a close friend at the Embassy, sat on the plane next to me and almost blew my cover, when she put a pillow under her dress to look like me. As I walked up and down the aisle in the plane to stretch, Marissa followed me with the pillow tucked ostentatiously under her shirt!

Jim followed me to the States a week and a half later, arriving shortly before the baby was due. The morning after his arrival, we went to breakfast at a restaurant near our hotel, which had a nice buffet. All of a sudden I had to sit down and could not make it to the buffet to get food. I told Jim, "I think we need to get out of here!" Slowly and anxiously the two of us walked arm in arm the several blocks to George Washington Hospital, with me stopping every so often to double over with contractions. A car drove by full of local kids, and the father upon seeing us, yelled out, "Good luck, honey!" After a day and a night of contractions, our son Christopher was born. Jim proudly called all of our relatives and friends to tell them that his son at 23 inches long was "one-third of six feet tall." We had bought a tiny tee shirt with "Made in China" hand-printed across the front to put on baby Christopher.

As with so many women in the Foreign Service before me, I was left alone with my newborn infant when Jim had to fly back to China shortly after the christening. During this time, my ninety-five-year-old grandmother died. I took two-week-old Christopher across country to Ohio for her funeral, where new life and death came together. During the ensuing month on my own, I learned the essentials of mothering.

After six weeks of moving around with Christopher in tow, I flew for twenty-four hours back to China to reunite with the new father in Beijing. Managing things like how to nurse on the plane and how to leave my baby to go to the bathroom were all new challenges for me. While I was away, Jim had traveled with Ambassador Lilley to Xinjiang, the Muslim region in China's far west. In the ancient Silk Road city of Kashgar, he bought a little Uighur cradle with a hole in the bottom for baby boys to relieve themselves (I am not sure how girls managed). He bought lots of wonderful things to transform our apartment into a baby wonderland, filled with flowers and music, toys and colorful hangings.

With Mr. Li, our full-time cook, and babysitter Liu Ayi (Auntie Liu) to help, life was comfortable and I was able to enjoy being just a mother. Liu Ayi, a delightful woman from the rural hinterland northwest of Beijing, blessed us with a lovely smile all the time. Gentle and soft-spoken, she had raised several children of her own, which allowed her to help greatly to ease my path into motherhood. It was a privilege having the time to nurse Christopher and play with him without all the other distractions and duties that plague new mothers everywhere. When we did venture outside our little retreat, my little *waiguoren* (foreigner) baby drew lots of attention from the local people. People always wanted to touch and stroke him. Once when I tried to nurse him in a quiet corner beside the Great Wall, crowds of people gathered around and pulled at my blanket, staring wide-eyed, as if they had never seen a baby nursing before. My mother, who was visiting us at the time, intervened and tried gracefully to lure the crowds away by taking their photographs. But they persisted in commenting at how "even foreign devils breast-feed their little ones." There I sat helplessly, breasts exposed, providing the Chinese with a practical education about Westerners and their babies.

Our last two years in China following Tiananmen brought more forbidden contacts with our Chinese friends. Amazingly enough, our friends continued to brave the disapproving security gauntlet to visit us and share their feelings about what was happening in China.

In Beijing, we became friends with an older Chinese couple. They both spoke proudly of being Christopher's Chinese "grandmother" and "grandfather." We often went to their house for dinner and conversed for hours about developments in China. They welcomed us in their home and treated us like family. Grandma Han was an academic who made the most wonderful homemade dumplings, on which we feasted nonstop. Lao Liu, a retired senior Communist Party cadre, would show Jim party documents that he scoffed at and called "just propaganda." They told us endless tales of their harsh experiences during the Cultural Revolution.

During our time in China, we had the opportunity to meet three former American presidents—Nixon, Carter, and Bush—who came to China at different times to pay official visits. Meeting Richard Nixon was unbelievably strange for me. There I was, face to face with the man who had been the embodiment of the errors of the Vietnam War and against whom I had demonstrated on many occasions during my college years. What could I say to him?

"How do you like living in New Jersey?" was all I could stammer out as we shook hands. He responded kindly and intelligently about the state that we had in common.

Later, Jimmy Carter came to visit. Jim discussed peanut farming with him, arguing whether Carter's Plains, Georgia, or Jim's Dothan, Alabama, was the true "peanut capital of the world." At the embassy reception in his honor, President Carter walked around the Embassy compound with our son Christopher in his arms.

When a second "Made in China" child did not immediately materialize, we considered adopting a baby girl from the Qinghe orphanage, where I had been volunteering. In the end, however, we decided we were still too involved with Christopher to add another baby to our little family. I did, however, help embassy friends, the Meserves, adopt a little girl, whom they named Anna. In 1990, China was still very hesitant about letting foreigners adopt Chinese children. For them, it was a loss of face. The red tape and bureaucratic obstacles in the way of my friends' adopting Anna were truly monumental. In frustration, they went to the countryside and adopted another baby whom they called Lea. When Anna's adoption finally did come through, the Meserves left China with two little girls in their family. Twelve years later, I had the pleasure of hosting them at my home in the United States and meeting two lovely, grown-up American girls. It was remarkable for me to see them, realizing where they had come from—the huge impersonal orphanage in Yiheyuan. Today China has opened the doors for adoptive parents from all over the world, but in 1990 that was just beginning.

When Christopher was about six months old, Operation Desert Storm began with American bombs raining down on Baghdad. I would sit for hours in the rocking chair in our bedroom with Christopher on my lap, watching on TV as the bombs fell on Iraq in the distant war. We lived in a building with foreigners from many nations, including Iraq. Some days, we would be stuck in the elevator with Iraqis, as we descended ten floors in silence. I tried to look as non-American as I could and held my breath until we reached the ground. Although nothing untoward ever happened, it was most uncomfortable.

When Jim started talking about being posted to a new country, I found, to my surprise, that I was not ready to leave China. Perhaps like a caged bird, I had become accustomed to the routine and comfortable in my confinement. Dining with the new head of the Ford Foundation in China one night, I enthusiastically told him, "You're going to love it in Beijing, it's so interesting and colorful." He quipped in response, "You, my dear, have been here too long!"

When we departed China in the summer of 1991, I was a different person. I had learned so much about this ancient and complex culture just emerging from its decades of self-imposed isolation. During the three years we lived in Beijing, we watched the city change from a place where Mao jackets and Communist institutions predominated to a new and increasingly modern city, where young people dressed in smart suits and colorful miniskirts and high-rise luxury hotels abounded.

I hoped that I, in turn, had had some effect on the people I met and made some contribution to China, particularly to its disabled people and its women. I felt I helped some Chinese people understand more about the outside world and about Americans. Although China and Beijing were calm when we left, no one who was there during those years, including Jim and I, will ever forget what happened in Tiananmen Square.

China taught me to have patience and remain calm on the outside, to solve my emotional conflicts in private, to think of my community ahead of myself, to be proud of my ancestry and my country, to offer tea when I greet guests, to eat communally, to exercise daily in the open air, and to always bring gifts when visiting friends. Perhaps the most valuable lesson I learned, however, was that freedom is worth fighting for. I was fortunate enough to be from America, where democracy is the birthright of all citizens. Little did I know that as we boarded our plane to leave China, my dear friend and teacher, Lu Yong was trapped in a Beijing prison.

3
My Passage to India

In the summer of 1993, after we had reacquainted ourselves with American life for two years in suburban Washington, D.C., the State Department posted Jim to Madras, on the Bay of Bengal in the state of Tamil Nadu in South India. Just to ensure against boredom, we crammed three life-changing events into as many weeks: giving birth to the first girl ever in the Huskey clan, buying a new house, and moving to the far side of the world.

We were ready for the move, except that I was pregnant and due to deliver our much-wanted second child. In order to make our long-scheduled departure date, we decided to have our baby induced to assure that she and I had at least a few weeks of recuperation before the move. On July 23, I walked into George Washington University Hospital in downtown Washington, overnight bag in hand and feeling perfectly normal. Two-year-old Christopher yelled to me as I left the car, "Mommy, please don't give me a bald sister!" Within three short hours and with help from medical science, I gave birth to a beautiful, not quite bald, distinctly redheaded girl, with soft pale Irish skin and sparkling green eyes. We named her Caroline Meredith, after the North Carolina Meredith branch of Jim's family. The Alabama Huskeys were astonished, as no girl had been born to five generations of Huskeys. But there she was in all her glory, the newest member of our family about to face a huge adventure.

Soon after, at a scant four weeks old, little Caroline and her just-turned-three-year-old brother Christopher were both on a jet high over the Himalayas. My friends thought I was absolutely crazy. "This is off the stress charts," they cautioned, "buying a house, having a baby, and taking her at a few weeks old to live in far off India—all in one month!"

"At six weeks, I carried Christopher by myself to China. If I survived China, I can handle anything," I responded, with what turned out to be excessive bravado.

We arrived in Madras, later renamed Chennai, after thirty-nine hours of traveling with two babies in diapers and all their paraphernalia—car seats, strollers, diaper bags, snugglies, wipes, bottles, you name it. Disoriented by jetlag and baby overload and barely cognizant of what day it was, much less what city we were in, we arrived in hot tropical Madras, where Michael Keaveny met our family at the airport. An eternally upbeat Irish American, Michael had been assigned by the consulate to be our official sponsor and introduce us to life in India. He turned out to be truly a godsend and became one of our lifelong friends.

India—a bombardment, a deluge of the senses—hit me, the overconfident world traveler, like a ton of bricks. It is intense by every measure. To this Westerner, Madras at first glance was a sea of forbidding smells and strange sights. Sweltering August heat, clouds of mosquitoes, dust, dirt, and poverty all hit me in the face like a blast of hot air. It was also wildly colorful, teeming with life, chaotic and yet oddly wonderful. The morning after we arrived, Jim blithely went off to work at the imposing white U.S. Consulate on Anna Salai Road in the center of Madras, leaving me in an empty, cavernous house with no car, four-week-old Caroline and three-year-old Christopher. Thus began my life in India.

I had fully expected that China would have prepared me for India, but India was a shock to this girl from the northern climes of New Jersey. My Irish heritage had endowed me with skin that doesn't take well to hot sun, lungs that prefer cool fresh air, and a constitution that works best in moderate climates. India was the very opposite of these. The air was thick, heavy, and hotter than I had ever experienced. It hung on my body, closing in on me so that I feared I could not breathe. A terrifying claustrophobia seized hold of me.

I had grown up the eldest of five children in Livingston, New Jersey, a planned community designed with children in mind. India was about as far from orderly suburban Livingston as one can get. In India, life happens all around you—people living, worshipping, working, and sleeping in the chaotic narrow streets. Cows, sacred to

Hindus, wander freely about the streets. Hindu temples dotting the corners and alleys of Madras were filled with images of innumerable gods, ornately decorated with vibrant colors and gold leaf, oozing with the aroma of sandalwood incense. Strange *sadhu* holy men roamed the streets, their faces festooned with paints. Women languidly rustled past in their brightly colored, flowing brocaded or silk saris. Ox-drawn carts rumbled through the streets bearing piles of fruits and vegetables. Spicy odors, strong and pungent, wafted through the air. Bustling life in glorious color permeated Madras.

On our first morning in Madras, I awoke and peeked out of our new house into a sea of bobbing heads and eager eyes. Some thirty people were lined up in our driveway, all seeking a job with us. With my two small children in tow, I couldn't deal with interviewing so many needy people on my very first day. "Could you all please come back tomorrow?" I pleaded, not wanting to forfeit the opportunity to meet them. The many heads bowed gracefully in acquiescence and filed quietly out with hopeful thoughts. Not quite ready to venture into Madras's crowded main roads, I cautiously walked Caroline and Christopher in their baby carriage, carefully covered with mosquito netting, through narrow back lanes crowded with cows and people. Miraculously, we stumbled upon a nearby Western-style hotel, the Park Sheraton, and gratefully retreated into the coffee shop for a reprieve. As we drank cold milkshakes, Christopher mournfully looked up at me and asked, "Mommy, why are you crying?" Trying to nurse tiny Caroline in a dark corner seat of the coffee shop, I dishonestly replied, "Why, sweetheart, I am just so happy to be here." How could I explain to my three-year-old son how overwhelmed and lost I felt?

On first moving into U.S. embassy or consulate housing anywhere in the world, the houses feel like big empty warehouses. They all have the same imported Ethan Allen furniture—sometimes the very same pieces you had in your last post. The challenge is to convert this sterility into a home as quickly as possible. In India, the feeling of loss and emptiness was compounded by the fact that the house was truly cavernous, and for the first few weeks, we rattled around in it like loose change with just the few things we had brought with us in our suitcases. The air conditioners hummed continuously because of the sweltering heat, but they were old, noisy window units that drowned out conversation and music. The roar of these units made us feel like we were living in a factory. In this setting, sitting in a rocking chair under mosquito netting late at night, lonely and scared, I nursed Caroline with tears streaming down my face.

The incessant heat and humidity of those first few weeks in South India were oppressive. It was all I could do to resist the intense compulsion to grab the children, get on a plane, and go back home. I didn't know if it was postpartum depression, the shock of India, the heat, homesickness, or all of the above. I just felt trapped—by the heat, in my large empty house under yards and yards of mosquito netting; by the demands and constraints of nursing Caroline; by a crowded city replete with disease and poverty that I wanted to keep from my family; by the fact that all my possessions were in crates on a ship somewhere in the Arabian Sea headed for India; by the U.S. consulate's bureaucracy; by the then-still alien culture of South India—just trapped. The growing sense of claustrophobia was suffocating me.

I was unaware that I was dehydrated from nursing in the extreme, unremitting heat. My body began to shake and I couldn't sleep. I sat up all night holding my little baby tight. Jim had a hard time understanding me, although he tried. He expected me to be as happy and excited about our new post as he was. He had spent a memorable year in India a quarter of a century earlier and had fond memories of his stay in Madras. He went off each morning to his large air-conditioned American office on the fourth floor of the Consulate, while the children and I struggled to survive in the wholly new, alien culture of South India. I had to plunge into strange markets in search of food, hire a large household staff, stave off diseases, endure the heat, and learn to socialize with the warm and friendly but still distinctly different Madrasees.

Meeting Consul General Tim Hauser and his wife, Sandy, at a welcome luncheon in their home the day after we arrived caught me off guard. "So," they asked me, "how do you like it here in Madras?"

Gulping, I responded, "I know we are going to love it here," despite the large lump in my throat that took weeks to dissolve.

Christopher was sad-sacked, too, and longed for his life in America. One day he said, "Mommy, I don't know how to make my face smile. I miss Grandma." His words ran through me like an electric shock that doubled my longing for home.

The survival instinct forces expatriate spouses through the wrenching changes and isolation that we endure every few years, as we move from country to country. Each time we move, I am once again thrust into an unnerving, existential state, compelled once again to rediscover and redefine for myself the point of life. On the one hand, moving allows you to see things with a fresh perspective. On the other, without a clear purpose for being in the new place, it means confronting an abyss of the unknown, without a context for meaning. As the spouse of a diplomat, I have been constantly challenged to define what I will do in each post and discover how to find purpose and happiness in strange new cultures. This kind of challenge is extremely different from those faced by people who hold the same job, live in the same town, and sleep in the same bed year in and year out. It is a lonely process, calling upon all your inner resources.

My adjustment crisis reached a crescendo one night when we were at the home of our new neighbors, Barbara and Sandy. While dining, I felt panicky, as if I could not breathe. Although I hardly knew her, when I got in the kitchen alone with Barbara, in a panic attack I grabbed her and said, "I am not in good shape, I feel like I'm going crazy, you've got to help me!"

By coincidence and through luck, Barbara turned out to be a certified dance therapist. She took me by the shoulders, looked me straight in the eye, and said, "Calm down. I can help you. Come over to my house tomorrow morning and we'll start dancing."

Over the next few weeks, I danced my heart out, cried, and physically worked through my fear and loss. Barbara helped me sort through the feelings churning deep inside, and in the process saved me, and my marriage. Her gift of dance therapy ultimately enabled me to clear the fear and rubble from my heart and begin experiencing the remarkable wonders of India. It was a blessing to have Barbara next door.

After a while, another American consulate spouse, Martha Keaveny, Michael's wife, who was doing an amazing job raising three rambunctious little boys in Madras, helped shake me out of my doldrums, remonstrating, "What are you thinking? You cannot just get up and leave India! It is up to you to hold your family together. Come over to my house first thing tomorrow morning. Our kids can play together while you and I talk this through."

When we arrived at her house, Martha had organized a playgroup for Christopher, her boys, and some other expatriate children. Her house, brimming with American toys, food, and television tapes, was a haven where we happily retreated into our familiar American ways. Christopher and I immediately relaxed; like most creatures, we prefer what we are accustomed to. Often, in the first few weeks after you move into a strange new culture, a few familiar creature comforts or foods can make all the difference in the world.

Not long after that, Martha and Michael hosted a large reception to introduce Tim and Sandy Hauser and Jim and me to the social and business leaders of Madras. We were impressed by the great diversity of fascinating and gracious people in Madras. In one lovely night we met many of the major players in the city—writers, doctors, journalists, and business leaders, many of whom grew to become our good friends over the next three years.

One of the people I met that night was Dr. John, a traditional family doctor who began to come to our house and helped me straighten out my physical difficulties. Once he helped me realize that I was heat dehydrated and needed to adjust my liquid intake, I started to feel much better. Eventually, I hired a full household staff of seven endearing people, who in turn began to introduce us to South Indian customs, and helped us set up a beautiful home that made our family feel comfortable. I have always found that once our house begins to feel like a home, full of color and our favorite things, we can begin venturing forth with confidence, knowing we have a haven to return to as a reprieve from the strangeness of the country in which we are living. This home base provided us the safety net we needed to begin to take some risks and explore the intensity of India.

Our Secret Garden

Our rambling home and surrounding garden were set behind imposing white stucco walls. Flowers of every color draped the tall, whitewashed walls that buffered us from the outside world. From the back of the garden, a small archway led into the consul general's garden, with its swimming pool overlooking the lovely but often odiferous Adyar River. Adjacent to the pool was a clay tennis court, cared for by a wonderful slender barefoot man named Chandran, who played tennis like a pro and played with us on request. Jim played tennis with Chandran every morning at 5 a.m. to avoid the heat. Chandran always ran him into the ground, albeit gracefully, after which, dripping with sweat, Jim returned home to wake Christopher, Caroline, and me for breakfast on the terrace.

Another archway led from the left of our garden to the wonderful old whitewashed Madras Club, the heart of colonial British India, on the banks of the Adyar River. The river flowed by our house and the Madras Club, past the exotic grounds of the Theosophical Society, and emptied into the Bay of Bengal.

Madras is a large city that had been the capital of British India in the eighteenth century. It is foremost a beach town, with a long oceanfront running the length of the city. Despite the heat, there is almost always a slight ocean breeze that clears the air and cools the city. Sadly, the South Asian tsunami in December 2004 killed thousands of people along that stretch of beach.

Deep fuchsia-colored bougainvillea arched over the gate to our house and covered our patio in an arbor of brilliant purple. A glass-enclosed terrace wrapped around the outside of the house, where our cook, Leela Auntie, served breakfast to us every morning. Allowed a budget by the consulate to reupholster the furniture in the large living, dining, and study areas, we turned to the rich Indian fabrics, seeking to bring the vibrant chartreuses, oranges, and reds of India into our daily lives. An upholsterer set up his sewing machine right in our living room, where it buzzed for several weeks, gradually transforming our house into a home full of warm Indian color. The children's playroom was brightly adorned with soft Indian toys and pillows. Richly hued draperies and chairs completed the Indian flavor in our living room.

Upstairs was a large central family room, encircled by the children's bedroom, a large master bedroom with a wraparound, screened-in balcony overlooking our huge garden, and a study. Taking showers, while looking out onto our lush tropical foliage, it slowly began to hit me that we were living in an enchanted out-of-the-way place. That it was far from the hustle and bustle of the east coast of the United States, or the world for that matter, disturbed me at first, but with time that was what made life there so charming.

The kitchen of our Madras house was the domain of the household staff. The pantry was stocked with food we shipped from the United States, as well as local spices cumin and cardamom, curry and cloves. One of the first staff I hired was Leela Auntie, a sweet portly grandmotherly woman with extensive experience as a cook. She was the boss of the kitchen, in charge of buying the food, planning the menus, feeding the staff, and cooking delicious meals for us. Occasionally we felt homesick for American-style food, so she learned how to cook Western recipes for us. She made fresh pureed baby food for Caroline from vegetables she bought at the market and wonderful cakes for me. Through Leela Auntie, we all came to greatly enjoy Indian cuisine. Caroline and Christopher grew up loving to eat curries, dahls, chutneys, chapattis, rotis, idilies, and other Indian delights.

Our children were fortunate to grow up among a retinue of loving Indian "aunties" and "uncles," as we called them, who buzzed about our house, making sure it all functioned harmoniously. Each person who worked for us had a different job, in part reflecting the intricacies of the draconian caste system. Leela Auntie, the cook, did not clean, but was a loving "grandma" to our children. Youthful Jaya Auntie, our lovely baby ayah, lit up our days with her beautiful smile and played games with the children. Our driver, called S.P., was my constant support and protector, helping with errands, not only driving but also often translating our needs into Hindi or Tamil. Sampath, our tall, gentle gardener, made our lives magical by his thoughtfulness. Shuganah, our "outside sweeper" (who never entered the house) was so appreciative of the wrap-around saris we bought for her, and marvelous Mary Auntie, the inside housekeeper (who would never work outside), gracefully took efficient care of the entire household, creating calm and greatly easing our lives. Our gate guards, Ramalingam and Murali, protected the compound and doted on our children. These seven people who worked for us formed their own little community and provided us a wonderful life.

Managing this extended "family" kept me quite busy. In India you are not just an employer but also the patron of your employees. You provide for their health, their meals, their clothing, their housing, and their families and help with their emotional problems. It was a full-time job, and I often got far too involved in their lives. My new friend, Ranjini, whom I met through a baby group I formed, warned me again and again, "Joanne, don't get so involved in their lives. It is better to remain more detached and objective."

In typical American fashion, however, I was always worrying about their families and helping them with their problems. In fact, our interaction with our Indian staff greatly enriched the texture of our own lives. We learned the inside workings of their families, their struggles, their desires, and their beliefs. We went to their elaborate family weddings, helped out financially in times of need, and celebrated their Hindu holidays with them. Our children learned Indian customs and practices and did *pujas* to their gods. We all enjoyed the sense of harmony they brought to our house.

"*Vannakam*" Means Welcome in Tamil Nadu

India changes you if you don't resist its charm. The color, the smells, the clothing, the customs, the Hindu way of life with its hundreds of icons and rituals, in time all combined to transport me into a completely new frame of mind. But it was making Indian friends that finally absorbed me fully into India. South Indian people are unusually gracious, gentle, and welcoming. We made many wonderful close friends. South Indians love to entertain, and do so in elaborate and wonderful ways. It was these most hospitable people who introduced Jim and me to the complex and wonderful South Indian culture.

When we first moved to Madras in 1993, few foreigners were living there. Only twelve Americans worked in the U.S. consulate, and there were no American businesses. Several consulate officers' wives fled Madras, unable to cope with the extreme heat, poverty, and inability to work. Leaving had devastating consequences for their marriages. I was one of those who chose to stay, in part because of my Indian friends. They enjoyed meeting Americans and regularly wined and dined us.

Our lives were fun and stimulating, socially and intellectually. Most of the Madras elite are highly educated, sophisticated, and well traveled. We enjoyed frequent discussions of political and economic affairs, U.S.-Indian relations, and political and economic developments in South India. These were lively times in Tamil Nadu. We always had stimulating talks about Jayalalitha, the movie-starlet-turned-chief-minister of Tamil Nadu, who led a most public and unconventional lifestyle. Gaudy posters of her gazed benevolently down on us at every street corner. She maintained her movie star aura, and the Indian masses revered her like a goddess, providing endless conversation fodder among the disapproving elite. Her boyfriend, MGR, had been a Bollywood star and preceded her as chief minister, thus establishing the link between stardom and politics.

One of the first times Jim and I were invited to an Indian home, our hosts had nonchalantly suggested, "Just drop by. It will be a casual gathering of only a few friends." Being American, we took them at their word and prepared for a small backyard barbeque. When we drove up their long driveway, elegantly framed in white lights, we found 150 people circulating around a swimming pool, women dressed in flowing silks and satins, men in white dinner shirts, all dining to a fully catered evening of wine and South Indian music.

"This is what they call casual?" Jim asked.

"Thank God, I didn't wear my cutoff jeans!" I sighed.

Thereafter, we dressed up for all parties, of which there were many. Socializing in Madras was done on a grand scale, with live music, lighting, color, and lively conversation. Parties usually began around 9 p.m. and often went on until midnight or later, at which time a full, deliciously spicy South Indian dinner banquet would be served before the guests departed for home.

Art, music, dance, and politics were all intimate parts of our immersion into Madras. The state of Tamil Nadu, on India's southeast coast, is the cultural center for many distinct artistic traditions, all of which are deeply influenced by Hindu religion and culture. Karnatic music, for example, the chanting of Vedic poetry, is a highly sophisticated art form originating in neighboring Karnataka. The rearing of Brahmin and other high-caste children required knowledge of this musical tradition. The famous Kalakshetra School of Bharathanatyam Dance is located in Madras. Bharathanatyam is a highly stylized dance form in which well-known Hindu temple dramas are danced to hypnotic Indian music. Being a dancer, I loved to go sit in on classes and see performances in this wooden-domed school whenever I could.

Many leading schools of yoga also emanate from Tamil Nadu. Yoga is part of the everyday life of many Madrasees, who see it as one form of divine worship, rather than the huge commercial fad that it has become in the West. In my search for a place to study yoga, I ended up at a modest little white house that doubled as the school of Krishna Charia, a yogi with a large following in the West. One of his students, Iyengar, is himself well known in the West and has followers worldwide. Eventually I found a private teacher, a charming gentleman named Mr. Parthasarthay, who, at seventy, was in amazing shape. He came several times a week to our home and taught me yoga in the quiet of our study. It was a gentle, meditative way to experience India. In a more passive vein, I also found a masseuse who would come to our house each week and give me a full body massage with the pungent Indian avocado oil. This delightful luxury was something I looked forward to and, needless to say, greatly eased my passage to India.

Although I had worked in poor barrios in Nicaragua with the Peace Corps and in Harlem while in college, I found the poverty in India so pervasive and impenetrable that I felt I could not get involved in the extremely poor sections of the city, either working or volunteering. Instead, I turned my energies to sharing my experience of working with special education.

At the invitation of Indian friends, I joined the International Women's Association (IWA) and through them formed a Very Special Arts committee to work with disabled people in Madras. When I was director of Very Special Arts International at the Kennedy Center in Washington D.C., I spent eight years traveling the world and training special educators to use the arts for educating and rehabilitating children with disabilities. In China I continued this work. In India, through IWA, I met Nanditha Krishna, a remarkable and elegant writer, anthropologist, and philanthropist. Her enthusiasm spurred me to secure a grant from the U.S. Information Agency to bring a group of talented artists from America to train special education teachers in Madras. Nanditha helped me organize a two-week training program for special educators, where we demonstrated how to adapt arts to work with deaf, blind, and physically disabled people. At the workshop, these artists focused on the uses of music and the visual arts. I taught how to make theater available to the deaf by using visual cues, and techniques for wheelchair dancing for physically disabled people.

The lovely and brilliant Nanditha was part of a large Brahmin family that had lived in Madras for centuries and was deeply engaged in a wide variety of philanthropic projects. During our work, she and her mother, Shakunthala, who together had written many books on Hindu culture, helped me to begin to understand the vastly complicated Hindu religion and culture.

With other friends, I started going to Indian temples and learning about the innumerable Hindu gods. Hindus have a different manifestation of god for each aspect of life. They have specific gods for education, good luck, wealth, health, fertility, and so forth. One of my favorite gods was Ganesha, the portly, mischievous Elephant God, who represents good luck. Elephants, in fact, are sacred in India and many temples have live elephants living on the grounds. A visit from an elephant was an auspicious sign. A large temple elephant occasionally lumbered with his trainer to our house bringing sacred blessings to us in our own driveway. Painted in swirls of intricate colors, our neighborly elephant would bop each of us lightly on the head with his trunk as a blessing. We would sometimes climb up on his back and ride around the garden. Christopher and Caroline became accustomed to the visiting elephant, and the staff would never miss the opportunity to be blessed. In India, every moment is a chance to worship the divine. So much so, that once, when our gardener, Sampath, found a live cobra in our yard, he refused to kill it, much to our dismay, because, like most Indians, he saw the serpent as a sacred creature.

As I grew to know and love India and things Indian, I started wearing Indian clothes. Salwa chemise, a long tunic top over baggy pants, and saris, nine meters of silk wrapped around the body, are all fun to wear. I gradually put aside most of my Western clothes, which began to feel clunky, dark, and boring at Indian parties. A gray or blue suit that seemed great in Washington looked absolutely stiff and drab among gracefully and colorfully dressed Indian women. It was a pleasure wearing the flowing silks of South India, which come in brilliant fuchsia, orange, chartreuse, and purple. Once I put on a sari, I felt transformed and infinitely more feminine. But a sari is not easy to put on. You have to wrap the many meters of silk around and around your body, then drape it in prescribed ways, tucking it in without any pins or other support. Finding it impossible to put on a sari by myself, I always had to ask our baby ayah, Jaya, to assist me. Venturing out, I was forced to move with grace, taking small steps and sitting upright with elegance, all the while fearing the whole thing would unravel and fall off and Jaya wouldn't be there to put it back on! Grace is what all of South India has that we in the West sometimes lack. South Indians are a gentle people. They wear jasmine in their hair, smile often, take their time, move quietly, and pray to the gods for everything. I knew I had much to learn from them.

Enchantment

One of our family's favorite people was our playful gardener, Sampath. He delighted in enchanting our children's lives, often surprising them with gifts of small animals. Cages of lovebirds, tanks of fish, a bunny, and even a chameleon all came to us from Sampath. One day he brought two large, beautiful green parrots to Christopher, one with a ring around an ankle, and the other without. Christopher named the ringed parrot "India" and the other "America."

Christopher spent hours watching India and America in their cage, trying to teach them to talk. They squawked back and Christopher, in his naiveté, thought they were saying they wanted to be set free. Sampath said sadly their wings had been clipped, so they could never fly away. So, thinking it was safe, Christopher opened the cage door. Cautiously India and America ventured out, at first onto a nearby branch, then around the garden. Christopher would walk around for hours with India and America, one on each shoulder. One day, America was nowhere to be found. Christopher and Sampath looked everywhere for him. Perhaps, Christopher surmised, America's wings grew back and he flew home to America. But India, he said confidently, would never leave, because she was already home. India stayed with us for quite a while, perched in the bougainvillea by the door. But freedom was too hard to resist and one day, she, too, spread her wings and flew away. Perhaps she still lives in India, or perhaps she reunited with her dear friend, America.

One Easter, I asked Sampath, "Would you like to be the Easter bunny for my children?"

"Yes, Madame, I would be pleased to do so," he politely responded, though he had never even heard of the Easter bunny in Hindu India.

On Easter morning, with all the consulate families assembled in the garden for an Easter party, Sampath arrived in a three-wheeled auto rickshaw, dressed in a white rabbit costume, which I had rented. Inside the rickshaw, he had transported baby chicks, bunny rabbits, several small goats and lambs—a virtual petting farm for Caroline, Christopher, and the other children. The children could not believe their eyes when they saw the huge Easter bunny and all of the animals spilling out of the auto rickshaw. Sampath was truly our "magic man," as we called him in those days.

At Christmas, Sampath draped lights and decorations he hand-made throughout our garden making it into a virtual fairyland. Though he was thoroughly Hindu, he built a Christmas crèche out of wood and straw and hung stars in it. Everything he did seemed to have a touch of magic. Laughing, Sampath entertained and glee-fully danced with the children whenever he could.

Interestingly enough, Hindu Sampath had no qualms about celebrating Easter or Christmas. The tolerant Hindus have no problem accepting Jesus as God. Hinduism is an accepting religion, with room for all things holy. Jesus, Buddha, and Mohammed can exist alongside Shiva and Vishnu. I noticed that Jaya hung pictures of these various deities in her room and paid daily homage, doing pujas to all of them.

Sampath and Jaya took Caroline out to pick flowers daily and returned to make wonderful displays of brilliant flowers floating in water basins, which they placed around our front door. In the driveway, Jaya also drew *coloms*, elaborate designs with brilliant colored rice flour that provided a beautiful and elegant way of greeting our guests. You could feel the enchantment in the air as loving glances were exchanged back and forth between Jaya and Sampath, while our children ran around them giggling and delighted. There was happiness in the air and life on our compound was harmonious and joyful in those days.

Brahmins and Untouchables

One evening, after we had been in India about a year, a stranger knocked on our door, told us he was Sampath's brother, and simply said, "Sampath has killed himself!"

Disbelieving, Jim and I immediately drove to Sampath's house, a small dirt-floor hut, which we found empty, except for a few clothes we had given him that were folded neatly in the corner. The new pair of Nikes we gave him for Christmas stood by the door and one of Jim's shirts hung on a hook, otherwise there was nothing. His body lay on the dirt floor, still and alone. None of his family or neighbors knew why he had hanged himself. Was it for lack of money? Why didn't he ask us for help? Was it because Jaya had spurned him? Could she have broken his heart so badly? Was it because he was in some trouble we didn't know about? Did he actually kill himself? People surrounded his hut, wailing and crying. In the sea of pushing, grief-stricken neighbors, I cried my heart out. Such a gentle soul—gone. Our magic man—gone. I looked into the surrounding faces, all poor beyond my experience, all crying, all hopeless. He was one of them, one of India's dalits, once called "untouchables," but renamed by Gandhi "Children of God." His friends told us Sampath had money problems and, maybe, also love problems.

We never learned the full story, but I loved that man, and I believe he had a special spirit. I will never forget him; his spirit still lingers with us.

That night, I was full of sadness as I told our young children that Sampath had been killed in an accident while riding home on his bicycle. Some day we will tell them the truth of his death. We still, to this day, talk about him, about the wonderful, gentle Sampath, who graced our lives for a short time. We are grateful that we had the opportunity to know him—the poorest of the poor, but so rich in spirit.

After we left Sampath's hut that night, Jim and I went to yet another social event at one of the homes of a wealthy Indian friend. It was difficult to make sense of the vast difference in lifestyles, the extremes of wealth and poverty. Feeling nauseous in the presence of such opulence and gaiety, I told Jim, "We have to leave now. My heart is broken over Sampath." We went home in silence, not able to comprehend.

This extreme contrast between rich and poor was one of the most difficult things for me to come to terms with living in India. Indians live side by side, rich and poor, with seemingly little resentment and violence, as opposed to the anger that exists in many other cultures where this kind of disparity is present. Hinduism, except for the radical nationalistic Hindutva variety, teaches a kind of acceptance that is India's saving grace. With over a billion people living in close quarters, the peace is kept by this acceptance of one's place in life, as defined by the Hindu social order. After Sampath's death, I was much more aware of the rawness and fragility of the lives of Indians living at the bottom of the social structure.

Christopher, who was three years old when we moved to India, started attending an Indian Montessori preschool. Called Abacus, it was run by Kamini Sundaram, the daughter of our good friends, Comi and Gopi, in whose garden the school was located. Gopi was a highly cultured and widely traveled gentleman, who loved to play tennis and cricket and hunt for wild animals. Adorning the walls of his home were the heads of game he had caught in India and Africa, especially in Botswana, Namibia, and Tanzania. Gopi's granddaughter, Magdalika, became one of Christopher's best friends. Christopher was one of only two American children at the school. Taught by Joy Auntie and Jayshree Auntie, two gentle, caring teachers who spoke softly and wore gorgeous flowing saris, Christopher learned about Indian holidays and history in the simple thatch-roofed school, set high on stilts in a garden filled with flowers and flame trees. The students took off their shoes as they entered the classroom, while monkeys frolicked outside from tree to tree. Parents became close friends as they waited together each day by the gate for their preschoolers to come running to greet them. Christopher, in his red and white checkered uniform, would run with his Indian classmates down the steps of the tree house–like school room, past the red flame tree blossoms and the mothers in their saris, into my arms. During the monsoons, the garden would completely flood, so that we had to wade barefoot in water up to our ankles and hop from stone to stone to get through the schoolyard. I loved going to that school, with its uniquely Indian aura.

Through the school, we met a fascinating set of friends who further introduced us to India. Sangeetha and Ranga, the parents of Sharon, one of Christopher's friends, became close friends. They lived in an apartment above Parthananda, a beloved guru, who dressed in long orange robes and had many followers. Each time I went to visit her for our baby group, I found the guru's followers lined up in the hallway waiting to talk with him and receive his teaching and blessing. After a while, Sangeetha arranged for me to meet with the guru to discuss my own spiritual growth and learning. This was something that many Indian people do regularly as part of their daily lives, but for me it was a different and enriching way to think about life's meaning.

Mukund, the father of Vinaya, another of Christopher's friends, was a journalist with the *Indian Express* newspaper at the time, then later with *The Hindu*. Our family traveled with them to his home state of Kerala, where we enjoyed a week exploring the wild and deep tropical forests of South West India and encountering elephants. Kamini and her husband, Aryama, the founders of Abacus School, were also friends. We enjoyed many colorful evenings dining at their home, while our children played together for hours. Jim organized a weekly soccer game for all the children, and every

Saturday morning their families came to our garden to socialize and watch while Jim coached the children in how to play soccer.

The Madras Club, the once-*pukka* (whites only) British colonial club that stood next door to our house overlooking the Adyar River, was a remnant of times long gone. The whitewashed buildings housed a dining room, ballroom, bar, billiards room, and a grand terrace that wrapped all around. Once, an off-limits bastion of British colonialists, it was now run by the Indian elite. An exclusive atmosphere still pervaded the old building. The waiters wore white turbans and starched white shorts. Every afternoon, Christopher on his bicycle, Caroline in her carriage, Jaya, and I, walked past rows of bougainvillea that embraced the club gates. We passed the tennis set in their whites playing on clay courts and joined the other mothers, foreign and Indian, at the old-fashioned playground adjacent to the swimming pool. The children scurried around collecting yellow flowers for us and played in the sandbox, as we sipped lime sodas in the warm sultry early evening air. In contrast to China, I found it amazingly easy to make Indian friends. Through my children, I met Ranjini, Sangeetha, Rohana, and others with whom there seemed no cultural barrier separating us. That most educated Indians speak "the Queen's" English, albeit with a delightful Indian lilt, facilitated our communication and understanding; but it may have been the shared bond of motherhood that transcended cultural differences.

Year in and year out, we sang Christmas carols, acted in plays, and danced at formal Scottish balls in the grand Madras Club ballroom. Every New Year's Eve, yellow lights were draped over the trees around the club creating a soft glow that floated in the warm night air. Most of the social and industrial elite of Madras, dressed in their finest attire, gathered on the terrace to greet each New Year. At midnight all crowded onto the dance floor, and at the stroke of midnight, hundreds of balloons fell from the vaulted ceiling as we kissed each other on both cheeks. Here, there was a sense of tradition that went back a century or more, when life was simpler. It is so rare in our modern fast-paced Western world, and yet, for a few moments each year there was a special feeling of camaraderie and graciousness at the Madras Club. I could not imagine a more perfect place in the world to be on New Year's Eve than in the Madras Club with friends. When we first moved to

India, I was most bothered by the thought of being so far from the "Western world." After living in Madras for a while, however, it was the very slow, gracious, almost other worldliness of my Indian life that I grew to cherish.

Partly because of our status as foreigners, there seemed few barriers to getting involved in almost everything in Madras. With few Westerners in Madras in those days, theater opportunities abounded and a little talent went a long way. I had worked as an actress before, but in Madras it was easy to be a star. Opportunities came for me to film television commercials, star in plays, cabarets, dances, and pantomimes. For a gala evening of the International Women's Association, I was able to produce a show called *The Woman of Today*. I played lead roles in Neil Simon's *Plaza Suite* and Oscar Wilde's *The Importance of Being Ernest*, entertaining Indian audiences with the witty, though sometimes arcane, Western humor.

Art is a two-way street. I learned to appreciate the ancient Tamil Bharathanatyam dance. Originally performed in temples, bharathanatyam dances tell stories from the Bhagavad Gita, illustrating the tales through elaborate movements requiring great skill and discipline. The world-renowned Madras dance school, Kalekshetra, is a major center for the study of this dance form, with students coming to study from all over India and the world. I both learned from them and could share some of my Western experience with them—jazz, modern, and ballroom dance. Such cross-cultural mixing at every level of life, however folksy, is critical for understanding in our new global civilization.

Soon after we arrived in Madras, with Caroline just a few months old, Madras playwright Tim Murari asked me to star in his new play *Lovers Are Not People*. This was a humorous play about a wife who catches her husband cheating and skillfully uses subtle charm, rather than anger, to win him back. "I am sorry, but, I can't be in a play now, since I am still nursing my baby," I responded disappointedly. Miriam, the director replied, "Oh yes, you can. We'll hold the rehearsals at your house!"

Being in a play is a great way to meet everyone in town. When *Lovers* was performed at the Taj Hotel for local Madras audiences, I became known in Madras as the woman who won her philandering husband back. In real life, my husband was waiting off stage, holding our baby, Caroline, so I could nurse her between acts— an American way to keep your husband around!

Citibank invited me to dance for a television commercial entitled "East Meets West at Citibank." An Indian dancer and I choreographed a dance merging Western and Indian dance traditions. Hilariously, when I arrived at the studio to film the commercial, however, there was a Swan Lake tutu waiting in the dressing room for me to wear. "There is some confusion," I laughed, "I am certainly not a ballet dancer, but a jazz dancer, with a dance style quite different from classical ballet." We worked through these misunderstandings and in the end, produced a global-minded commercial that incorporated Western jazz and bharathanatyam and ran regularly on local television stations for over a year.

Filming a movie or commercial in India is quite an adventure. India produces more films each year than does Hollywood. In fact, Bombay (now Mumbai), the center of the Indian film industry is known as Bollywood. As the second major film center in India, Madras, which is located in Tamil Nadu state, is known as Tallywood and has a number of large film studios. Because of the sweltering heat and lack of air-conditioning, the studios do much of their work in the cool hours of the middle of the night. I usually arrived around eleven p.m., and worked through the night until six a.m. The movie studios are huge, with hundreds of people running around—dancers in garish costumes, singers, crew, and stagehands. People roamed in and out of my dressing room doing my hair, makeup, and costumes. With labor relatively cheap, there are numerous people to do everything—while one would fan me with huge hand-held fans between shots, others crawled around the scaffolding, moving lights and shifting props. Waiters brought delicious South India food during breaks, and sound technicians heaved microphones overhead. Indian films often involve huge scenes with hundreds of people singing and dancing. Cecil B. DeMille would have been impressed by the scale of movie production in South India! I certainly was. Only in recent years, however, have Western audiences started to become familiar with Indian films, such as *Monsoon Wedding* and *Bombay*.

Surprisingly, some Westerners living in Madras complained about the lack of things to do, although almost anything was possible. With costs so low, one could do things on a grand scale. All it took was ingenuity and imagination to make things happen.

Global Adjustments

As we were experiencing South Indians' welcoming graciousness and interest in the United States, the traditionally leftist Indian press constantly criticized the United States for imperialism and for imposing its nuclear nonproliferation standards on India. The Indian press portrayed the United States as a hegemonic superpower that sought to lord it over other nations. It criticized American arrogance and accused us of trying to control what India could and could not do. How dare the United States prevent India from having nuclear arms, the papers complained, particularly since the United States is the largest nuclear power in the world? Despite the fact that Jim was an official representative of our government, I have to admit that I understood their logic. Since I was not working for the U.S. government, I could freely express my opinions without having to worry that my words might end up in the press the next day. Jim, on the other hand, was always aware that everything he said could be construed as official U.S. policy. Many of our friends were Indian journalists, and sometimes Jim's casual comments did end up in the press, but fortunately without negative consequences.

We had arrived in India in the fall of 1993, soon after India began to liberalize its old top-heavy Nehruvian socialist economy. Indians desperately wanted to develop economically and knew that their country needed to engage with the rest of the world, including the United States. At the time, Indians had something of a love-hate relationship with the United States, clinging to leftist criticism of American imperialism while clamoring to send their sons and daughters to the United States to study. Prime Minister Narashima Rao understood that opening up the economy was the key to India's future. He tried to make it attractive for foreign businesses to invest in India. As the consulate's political-economic officer, Jim kept Washington informed about developments in the four South Indian states of Tamil Nadu, Karnataka, Andhra Pradesh, and Kerala and helped facilitate the inflow of U.S. business into South India.

It occurred to me that international business representatives moving to India might experience the same kind of adjustment troubles as I had. If Western businesses were considering moving to India, they would be concerned about how their employees and their families would adjust to the strange and unique environment of India. This conceivably might be a deterrent to their coming at all. With my friend, Ranjini Manian, whom I had gotten to know through the baby group, I explored the idea of starting a consulting business to help international business people invest and possibly live in India. With her long experience as a travel agent associating with Americans and Europeans living in Madras, Ranjini agreed on the need and was game to go into business together. We decided to name our business "Global Adjustments" and chose as our business motto the tag line "Easing Your Passage to India." Ranjini luckily had a flat she was not using at the time, and within days we had literally hung out our sign and found ourselves suddenly in business.

Our objective was to attract foreign businesses and facilitate their moving into South India. We organized Global Adjustments to take care of every need they might have—housing, schools, doctors, household and business staff, cars, furniture, and appliances. We held orientation meetings to teach about South Indian culture, including how to eat Indian style and the complex intricacies of Indian social and business protocol. We hosted "A Taste of Madras" at the Chola Sheraton Hotel, and invited businesses from Madras to participate and introduce expatriates to the delights of Madras, a city that I had already learned to know and love. A host of local vendors put on spectacular displays of regional silks, food, crafts, and services, for Westerners to view and sample.

When we arrived in Madras in the early fall of 1993, there were few international businesses in the city. Soon after Global Adjustments opened for business, however, Ford Motor Company began weighing whether to build an assembly plant in Pune, near Bombay, or in Madras. Ford executives paid a visit to Global Adjustments. Ranjini and I showed their CEO, John Parker, around Madras, visiting schools, hospitals, clubs, and residential neighborhoods. We emphasized the color, texture, and beauty of the city but may have played down problems with infrastructure and daily inefficiencies. We assured him that Global Adjustments could help make Madras comfortable for his employees and their families.

Parker asked me in front of his staff, "Do *you* like living in Madras?"

I replied with full honesty, "Yes, I do very much."

"Look at that face," he said turning to his colleagues, "Do you think she would lie to us?"

Ranjini and I both played an indispensable part in getting this bicultural business off the ground and running. It was important, on the one hand, that expatriate spouses and children could ask culturally sensitive questions to a fellow foreigner, such as: Will I get sick? Why do Indian people wear bindis (red dots) on their foreheads? Why do people urinate in the streets? These and others questions they would have been embarrassed to ask an Indian, but I was there to answer them.

At the same time, Ranjini was essential to the success of the partnership. A native of Bombay, she exuded graciousness, warmth, and sophistication. She had married into a Madras Brahmin family with many connections. Her mother-in-law was a Karnataka singer and her husband, Chinu, a prominent businessman in the construction industry. Having previously been a travel agent in the city, Ranjini knew Madras inside out and knew how to get things done in the Indian manner. She dealt with the city government, real estate agents, banks, travel agencies, and school administrators. A world traveler herself, she was the perfect partner for this business.

Having had such a difficult adjustment myself, I knew what Westerners needed to enable them to relax and feel confident before they could enjoy India. One of the greatest joys of living in Madras was forming friendships with South Indian people. Ranjini and I, with our evident friendship, were able to excite clients about the richness of South Indian culture and life.

Ranjini and I worked hard to attract clients, at times feeling almost like prostitutes, waiting in international hotel lobbies to hand out our brochures. Several months after we opened shop, we finally received two contracts—one with cellular phone giant Airtouch International, and the other to help Ford Motor Company move its employees to Madras. This was just the break we needed for our new business. Ford, having chosen Madras over Pune, would be moving many foreign families to Madras over the next two years. We literally held the hands of incoming families, helping them feel secure and learn about life in Madras. We set up survival shopping tours, city tours for kids, and courses on Indian culture, cuisine, and business etiquette.

Ford's decision to come to Madras in turn inspired Hyundai and other automobile- related industries to move to the city. Global Adjustments was in the right place at the right time, or more accurately, I would like to think, helped make Madras the right place at the right time. After I departed Madras for Kenya two years later, Ranjini continued to run Global Adjustments, which has now become a highly regarded business throughout India and a main-stay of Madras/Chennai, which has become a truly international commercial center with many expatriates. Today, fourteen years later, I remain their North American representative; and in Global Adjustments literature, Ranjini still graciously mentions me as her co-founder. The business has expanded to six cities in India and has sixty employees.

In the interim years, India has become a leading partner in the international market, providing outsourcing to companies throughout the world. This provided a parallel program develop-ment for Global Adjustments (GA) in that Indian business people needed to understand Westerners. "They seem so rude." "Why are they always in a rush?" they would ask. "They are so concerned about timelines and production. Do they even care about our families?" We tried to assure them, "Westerners are certainly concerned about efficiency and the corporate bottom line, but they're also really warm and friendly people and would love to learn about your families."

GA designed a program called, the Global Indian, to train managers of Indian companies in Western management styles and business etiquette. To demonstrate the difficulties in communicat-ing across cultures, Ranjini and I opened our Global Indian seminars with short skits in which I played the newly arrived Western manager and Ranjini the Indian partner. We dramatized in asides the private thoughts that ran through each of our heads as we met and greeted each other, making the cultural differences immediately visible and glaring. The Indian manager (Ranjini), for example, would ask me, "Would you like some tea?" I, playing the American manager, would turn my head to the audience and verbalize what I was really thinking, "I wonder if the water is boiled and filtered? I should reply no or I will get sick!" Then I would turn back to my Indian counterpart and say cryptically, "No thank you, I am not thirsty." Then the Westerner might ask, "Why do Indian women wear saris to the workplace, it seems so impractical!" The Indian partner would express to the audience what was really on her mind, "Women here wear saris, and have for thousands of years. What would you want them to wear—overalls?" Then she would turn to the Westerner and graciously explain, "Saris are actually quite efficient." The Westerner never understood what she was talking about. After a while, we would stop the skit and ask the Indian employees what problems they saw in this the first interaction between the Westerner and the Indian. This produced lively and productive discussions.

I would not have been able to teach this lesson had I not first learned about Indian culture myself. It had taken time, but I had come a long way. Too many businesspeople around the world don't take the time to understand the cultures in which they work. This missed opportunity leaves the world prone to anger and violence based on cultural misunderstanding. Personal interaction can help people transcend parochial ways of thinking and seeing the world and build understanding across cultural divides. Ranjini and I have become convinced that our kind of business, teaching cultural competency, is essential to survival in the modern global community.

As I worked with international businesspeople moving into Madras, it became clear that local Indian schools would not be able to handle a large influx of foreigners. At the same time, the absence of international schools was a disincentive for international business to consider setting up shop in Madras. Most Westerners want a "Western" education for their children, since they will eventually return home to finish school or go to college. Martha Keaveny led the way. Her husband Michael and I and a few other parents formed a committee to establish an international school in

Madras. The process was daunting. We needed to get advice on appropriate curricula, find a building, enroll enough students to pay for teachers, hire international teachers and an administrator, all of this without knowing whether we would be able to pay them. Martha worked long hours obtaining information and organizing the fledgling school. I served as vice chairman of the school board in charge of curriculum. For almost a year, we met regularly to plan the school. Ideas were bantered back and forth by the parents of prospective students. Slowly our school began to take shape. The American International School in New Delhi gave us administrative advice and curriculum materials, and the U.S. Department of State provided some funds to pay for books and other materials. Consequently, despite our multinational clientele, we decided to follow a strictly American curriculum.

In September 1995, the American International School of Madras (AIM) opened its doors with eighteen students, two of them our Christopher and Caroline. (The name has since changed to the American International School of Chennai, AISCH, which I have never thought was as fitting as AIM). Ironically, in those early post–Cold War days, the rooms we found to rent were in the Russian Cultural Center! The center was in desperate need of funds, since the Russian economy was failing. There could be no clearer statement that the Cold War had ended then the newly opened AIM.

On opening day we stood proudly watching the small band of international children enter their newly painted and furnished classrooms. One room housed five kindergarten children, including Christopher. Another room full of water toys, beads, and a sandbox housed the preschool that two-year-old Caroline attended. The playground, hand-built by Jim, sported colorful bamboo ladders tied to trees as the jungle gym, rope and tire swings, huge painted wooden crates for climbing, and an extremely popular tetherball that was the center of active competition for all the students.

The new school helped make Madras a major attraction for international business. When Hyundai arrived in Madras, they wanted to enroll 50 Korean children. The school had to adjust quickly to the growing demand for international education. In one year, AIM went from 18 to 60 students and continued growing over the following decade. Today, the American International School of

Chennai (AISCH) has a new $10 million building and more than 750 students. A major attraction for international businesses, the school has enabled the city to continue to develop and grow.

Beach Temples

Although we loved living in Madras, it was always nice to get away on weekends. Madras has a long wide beachfront, but the beaches are quite crowded and rather polluted. One of the joys of our life in Madras was a beach house we rented with the Keavenys, thirty miles south of Madras near the ancient temple town of Mahabalipuram. It was just a small compound of several thatched huts on stilts along a deserted stretch of beach, but it was our own and it was paradise. Getting away on the weekends, we felt the freedom of sun, sand, and ocean. There were almost no other people on that stretch of pristine beach. We rented the huts from an Indian artist and her German boyfriend, who respected our privacy and we theirs. On several occasions, Michael Keaveny organized sunset dinners with full china and crystal, laid out on a table set right on the beach. There is nothing as delightful as dining with seawater lapping your toes, moonlight shining on your faces, and the sea breeze rustling your hair.

Our children loved going to the beach house, seeking interesting hiding places in the stilted huts, picnicking, and sleeping out under the moon. We spent many wonderful nights there, playing guitar and singing songs, telling stories, and making fires on the beach. We were guarded only by our English cocker spaniel, Jingles, who stayed by the bonfire while the ocean rolled in to the edge of our bed and the moon lit our hut.

Jingles had arrived our first Christmas Eve in India to a house full of visitors and a cypress tree decorated to recreate the feeling of Christmas in tropical South India. "All children should have a dog," Jim insisted. I was not exactly joyous about raising a puppy in India, where the many street dogs had rabies. But when Jim pulled into the driveway on Christmas Eve, in an attempt to sneak the surprise past the children and me and hide the dog under the Christmas tree, Caroline and Christopher ran out, and upon greeting Daddy caught sight of the little sandy-haired creature struggling to get out of the car. Christopher freed the tiny cocker and let her run gleefully around our garden.

"Let's call her Jingle Bells," shouted Christopher, "cuz she came on Christmas Eve, when Santa comes!" Thus, Jingles got her name. A diplomat's dog, she was totally spoiled, with steak for dinner, since imported dog food was expensive and hard to find. Caroline took charge of Jingles and played with her in the garden, dressing her up in costumes, wrapping her in baby blankets, pulling her in the red flyer wagon, and hiding her in the children's fort. Caroline and Jingles, with their matching ginger-colored hair, looked almost like siblings. Jingles grew up thinking she was the third child in the Huskey family. No one ever told her differently.

In August 1996, when Christopher was six and Caroline three, we prepared to leave Chennai. The evening before we left, I starred in Neil Simon's play *Plaza Suite* at the Park Sheraton Hotel, playing the mother of the bride in this raucous comedy. Many of our friends from across the city came to send us off by seeing the show. Ranjini had cajoled Air Touch International into hosting a lavish farewell supper-and-theatre evening. After the show, Jim and I went on stage and told our many Madras friends that we were not leaving forever, but promised we would be back one day. The newspaper theater reviewer wrote the next day that Madras had gotten two diplomats for the price of one. It was a sendoff we will never forget.

Madras, now Chennai, is today a fast-growing metropolis with many international residents. Without Global Adjustments and the American International School, perhaps many of the foreign businesspeople would not have moved to Madras. I am proud to have been a part of their founding. Both organizations are still actively operating and expanding along with the city and noticed by international businesspeople worldwide.

More important, however, had I left Madras early on during my difficult transition, I would never have learned to know and love India. Madras left Christopher, Caroline, Jim, and me with a lifetime of vivid memories. We slept under mosquito nets on hot sultry nights, wore flowing silks, encountered cobras in our garden, walked through rich tropical forests, and rode on elephants. We saw strange religious *sadhus*, visited temples filled with worshippers, performed pujas to the gods, and attended ornate weddings that went on for days. We learned to love the spicy delectable South Indian cuisine and worried about getting sick (but never did). We traveled on narrow roads full of people and animals, walked through crowded markets, and celebrated the many colorful Indian holidays. But best of all were the warm, lovely people of South India. We left with many wonderful friends in Madras and memories that will last a lifetime.

As we drove out of our driveway the last time, our whole staff—Leela, Jaya, S.P., Ramalingum, Mary, Murali, Shuganah—lined up to bid us farewell, all in tears. So were we. I can still see them standing there under the bougainvillea waving as we drove away, our hearts full of gratitude for all that we had learned and experienced, not knowing whether we would ever see them again.

I cherish the richness of Indian culture, the friendships, and my newfound understanding of one of the most ancient, cultured, and populous nations in the world. The struggles of India today, its determination not to be dictated to by the West, its political parties, the Hindu/Muslim conflict, arranged marriages, traditions, Hinduism, and so much more about that vital, culturally rich country are now more real to me. India changed me profoundly. Before I went to India, it was just a country of countless millions of poor people struggling to survive. After living there for three years and becoming enamored of the Indian culture in all its depth, I appreciate India's great wisdom. As the world shrinks, India will play an important part. Indians say "*Namaste,*" or "I honor the God within you." Because of India, I will try to remember that the divine is in all things, to smile more, and to honor the God within everyone I meet. I also hope that I will honor the differences between our nations and cultures. These differences are what make the world a wonderful and diverse place.

Southerner and Northerner, newlyweds
Joanne and Jim Huskey, 1986.

Joanne's Irish Catholic family, the Gradys, with Joanne seated
center, New Jersey 1990.

Young diplomats Jim and Joanne, U.S. Embassy Beijing, 1988.

Lu Yong, my Chinese teacher, Beijing 1988.

Chinese friends. Joanne at center, Lu Yong at far right, Beijing 1989.

Chatting with President Nixon, Beijing 1988.

Meeting President Carter, Beijing 1989.

Post-evacuation reunion—back in Beijing, Jim and Joanne, October 1989.

Made in China, evacuation baby Christopher, Beijing 1990.

Our Indian staff, Madras/Chennai, India, 1993.

Sampath, the Easter Bunny, Madras 1994.

Joanne and the temple elephant, Madras 1994.

Joanne with Jaya Auntie (at left), the Huskeys' baby ayah, and Leela Auntie, the cook, Madras 1994.

Big and small, Christopher with a temple elephant,
Madras 1994.

The Huskey family at the
Madras Club, Madras 1995.

Sampath, the magic gardener, with Christopher, in our garden, Madras 1995.

Joanne acting in an Indian film with an Indian film star, Madras 1996.

Global Adjustments Office, Joanne and Ranjini Manian, Madras 1995.

The cast of *Plaza Suite*, Joanne at far right, Madras, 1996.

4

Evolution, Creation, and Destruction in Africa

After three exotic years in India, we turned to our next posting. Peaceful, gentle India left us with a longing for warm tropical places. I had become accustomed to thriving on sunshine and now couldn't live without it. Returning to America at this stage in our lives would have brought pressure to return to work and leave my young children in order to survive financially—not an appealing option for Jim or me. Since most European posts are about as difficult to manage financially as Washington, the Third World—with its sunshine, warmth, household help, and outdoor living—beckoned.

We had never experienced Africa, and a political position awaited Jim in the U.S. Embassy in Kenya, a country that had always intrigued us. Nairobi once boasted a romantic and exotic reputation. By 1996, however, the rampant crime had tainted the once East African paradise. President Daniel Arap Moi had led his country to disaster through corruption. When I had visited Nairobi in 1985 to attend the U.N. International Conference on Women, the crime rate was already escalating. I never would have imagined that ten years later I would be going there to live. What, I wondered, would the crime be like at this point?

To assess life in Nairobi, I telephoned a few people who had worked at the Embassy there. I first called Linda, the woman, who held the job that Jim was considering. She quickly warned, "I may be the wrong person to ask, because of my negative experiences in Africa, but I have to be truthful." She related horrendous stories of her life in Kenya, including being robbed in her house by a gang of armed thieves, who stole everything and terrorized her family.

As a black American, Hutus thought she was a Tutsi on an official trip to Rwanda, during the upheavals and genocide there. They held her with a gun to her head and nearly killed her. Only her American passport, which she waved frantically in the air, stopped her would-be murderers.

"I am sorry to have to relay this, but I've had a terrible time in Nairobi. I should have left long ago," she said.

I hung up the phone and turned to Jim and said, "There is no way I am ever moving to Nairobi! It's way too dangerous!"

He suggested I call Alan Eastham, who had served as political counselor in Nairobi and was then political counselor in the U.S. embassy in Delhi. In contrast to Linda, Alan raved about Kenya and said he would go back there in a heartbeat. "Kenya was our best Foreign Service post; we had a wonderful time there—incredible, so much to do, and such a great climate. Our only regret is that we didn't stay longer!" he exclaimed.

Confused by such conflicting reports, and perhaps in a moment of madness, we accepted the posting, left behind our charmed life in India, and moved to Kenya. It was late summer 1996. Caroline and Christopher were three and six years old, and we packed them up and headed west across the Arabian Sea into Africa—to Nairobi.

Because of its position just south of the Equator and its mile-high altitude, Nairobi has cool, perfect weather—gorgeous hot sunny days and delightful fresh evenings. Most of the year, in the daytime, you can wear shorts and, because there are few insects leave the doors and the windows of your house wide open. In the evening, after sunset, it is cool enough to sit around a fire and relax. Perhaps this is why the British colonized Kenya—it was so refreshingly different from the damp, dreary weather in the UK.

The Huskeys arrived in Nairobi in early August of 1996. It was the perfect place for Caroline and Christopher, who were free to play outside all day long and not worry about putting on coats, jackets, or even shoes for that matter. Kenyan people do not have the colorful native clothes, music, and lifestyle common in West Africa, but rather sport a British-influenced Western look. They are easy going and friendly, always ready to welcome you by singing and dancing at official gatherings, their open smiles reflecting the warmth of the country.

On the streets of Nairobi, things were a bit more precarious. Unfortunately, in the first few weeks after arriving, because of the many reports I had heard, crime was uppermost on my mind. I was a bit skittish in public and distrusted almost everyone I met. The American embassy "security briefing," given immediately after we arrived, had warned us:

Don't open your car windows or you may be carjacked.
If you are held up at gunpoint, give them your car or whatever they want, or they might kill you.
Lock yourself in your safe haven [a barred cage around the upstairs of the house] at night, and always turn on your house alarm.
Don't let any strangers into your house.
Don't park in downtown Nairobi.
If you have a car accident, don't get out of the car or a riot might ensue!

In reality, it was necessary for the U.S. embassy to alert us to the dangers in Nairobi city, and we were grateful that the embassy tried to protect us. High walls surrounded our compound of four houses, with armed security guards at either end, and every window in our house barred for protection. Even our balconies sported prison-like bars! Because the Kenyan phone system was quite unreliable, we were given hand-held radios to keep with us at all times, which embassy Marine guards used for a weekly roll call. This may seem excessive. But though we started out uncertainly, in time, we got used to living within this security cocoon and accepted these restraints on our freedom as a fact of life in Kenya.

In our first days in Nairobi, however, when Caroline got sick, I reluctantly drove her to downtown Nairobi to see the embassy doctor, Gretchen McCoy. I did not know exactly where the Embassy was, and had to roll down my window to ask directions of complete strangers, wondering whether they were the ones I had learned about in the security briefing, who were going to point a gun at me and rob me. Meanwhile, Caroline opened the window on her side of the car and vomited, throwing all advice to the winds. I finally found the Embassy, but there were no parking spaces in the

Embassy compound. My radio call to the Marine on duty didn't help. When I anxiously asked him if I could park in the compound, he radioed back, "Negative."

"What do you mean, negative? Does that mean I have to leave?" I fearfully asked.

"Affirmative" came the answer.

So, contrary to the security briefing, I was forced to park on the street in downtown Nairobi and leave the car. Making my way to an empty lot in what looked like a war zone— strewn with garbage, mud holes, barbed wire, and broken glass–I anxiously left the car, climbed over barbed wire and through mud, and hurried through throngs of people, clutching Caroline in one hand and my purse in the other. All the while, the entire security briefing played like a bad tape over and over in my head. Extremely nervous with my sick daughter in tow, I was being forced by the embassy to break its own rules.

Entering the Embassy, Caroline and I went downstairs to the basement medical unit and promptly found ourselves trapped, locked in a long corridor with combination padlocks on the doors at either end. Security measures, by this point, were beginning to weigh heavily on my spirits. But this effort to find our way around the Embassy basement labyrinth would one day save our lives. When I finally arrived, harried, at the Medical Unit, the nurse on duty asked me, "Are you all right, Mrs. Huskey?"

I impolitely replied, "No, I hate this place and I wish I could go home now!" Thus began our life in Kenya.

As with our other posts, the culture shock of the first few weeks was overwhelming. It takes months to relax and find your stride.

A few days later, another embassy spouse gave me a tour of Nairobi. While parking in a supermarket parking lot, she casually explained that despite the crime, she always felt quite safe, because, she said, "I carry pepper gas with me at all times. Do you want to see it?"

She pulled it out of her purse and squirted a bit to demonstrate. Within seconds, the two of us were enveloped in gas and gulping for air. Gasping and choking, we clambered over each other to get out of her car. The pepper gas certainly worked, but I was not sure whom it was supposed to protect. At that moment, I decided not to take her up on using pepper gas, but, rather, to take my chances moving about the streets of Nairobi.

The Forest for the Trees

We soon discovered that the key to enjoying life in Kenya was to leave Nairobi city. Once out of Nairobi, Kenya is stunning in its physical beauty—vast open spaces in the savannah, dotted with spreading acacia trees, rolling green tea and coffee plantations in the highlands, the breathtaking Rift Valley, game parks with magnificent wildlife of every kind, and the coast, with its long stretches of white sand beaches, endless coral reefs, colorful tropical fish, and exotic Arab influence. I often felt the Kenyan countryside, with its vast diversity and color, was a hint of what the Garden of Eden must have been like.

One weekend early in our stay in Kenya, we drove our camouflage-brown four-wheel-drive Ford Bronco up Mount Kenya to Meru Mt. Kenya Camp for trekkers and climbers. Mt. Kenya is the highest mountain in Kenya at 17,058 ft. Only one mountain in Africa is higher—Mt. Kilimanjaro in nearby Tanzania. That day, we drove higher and higher through the forests on the slopes of Mount Kenya on dirt roads that rapidly deteriorated and eventually all but vanished. After a while, the boulders and loose mud before us had little resemblance to a road. Our car slipped and slid as we climbed and the engine finally just gave out on the steep incline, as the road disappeared.

Jim rolled back, trying to get the car into four-wheel drive, but while he held the driver's door open to look behind us, a tree we passed in reverse ripped the door off. We found ourselves stuck in the mud, high on Mt. Kenya, in the middle of a forest teeming with elephant, leopard, and buffalo, at 8,000 feet altitude as dusk began to settle. Luckily a Kenyan villager came walking by and gave us most welcome news—a little too welcome, it turned out. He said that the hikers' bandas (huts) were no more than a mile or two up the road. Since that seemed a manageable trek and it was beginning to get dark, I hastily set out walking with three-year-old Caroline and six-year-old Christopher. Dressed only in shorts and tee shirts and leaving Jim to salvage our car, we took sweaters and flashlights and walked in the gathering darkness through the forest up the mountain. The children and I walked for what seemed like forever with no sign of huts and plenty of signs of wild animals — elephant droppings, leopard footprints, and broken tree branches. It continued to grow progressively darker and colder, as we kept walking up the steep incline. My mind raced with visions of wild beasts and leopards in each tree. Christopher and Caroline bravely kept on going beside Mom, none of us admitting how frightened we were.

"When are we going to get there, Mommy?" they kept asking as the forest darkened.

"I'm not exactly sure, but we just have to keep walking," I whispered, trying to sound confident, while my heart pounded and my eyes darted frantically in search of wild animals.

Darkness fell. After walking for miles, there were still no huts. One foot in front of the other, with fear in our hearts, the children and I moved, shining our flashlights in the unforgiving darkness. After what seemed like hours, we heard an automobile engine in the distance—a Godsend. Headlights from behind finally came into view. Then the brown Bronco, with Jim sliding and wheel-spinning up the mountain in first gear, with the ripped-off door roped on, frantically came up behind us as we walked alone in the dangerous forest.

Overjoyed, relieved, and reunited, we scrambled into the car, just as the engine once again conked out. It looked as if we would have to sleep in our doorless car for the rest of the night. We thought about making a fire to keep warm, but then realized that fire might attract animals. Visibly worried, Jim tried over and over to crank the engine. After what seemed like ages, the engine suddenly caught and roared to life. We clambered in and Jim hit the gas peddle. We drove wildly up Mt. Kenya for another eight miles or so, not daring to slow down, until we reached the group of bandas (small huts), nestled in a field of wild buffalo. Of all the wild animals in Kenya, the buffalo is deemed the most dangerous, for they will attack and kill if threatened. We moved slowly through them holding our breath, to discover the last remaining empty cabin in the camp that night.

After we tucked Christopher and Caroline into their bunk bed, Jim and I heard footsteps padding across the cabin porch. It was a leopard, prowling outside our cabin. By this point totally exhausted, as we tossed and turned in our bed, we wondered how on earth we were going to get back down the mountain the next day. The only good news—at least it would be all downhill, 11,000 feet straight down.

From that first naïve trip, we learned that adventures in Kenya could be dangerous, even life-threatening. Later we heard stories of people lost in the forests of Mount Kenya, some of whom died and others who barely managed to survive. A year after our adventure, an American college coed visiting Kenya wandered from her group of hikers on Mt. Kenya, became lost, and remained lost for seven days. After a week of nonstop searching, a final search party, led by U.S. Consul General Julian Bartley, made one last flight by helicopter and miraculously spotted her, lying in a riverbed high up on the mountain, nearly dead. Luckily, she was brought to safety and reunited with her family in the United States. Hearing this and other tales, we vowed to be much better prepared for our future safaris.

Separating Theater from Reality

Wherever I live, I always seem to end up doing theater. In addition to loving it, theater offers a unique entrée into the society in which I am living. As an actor, I meet fascinating people and become drawn into the host culture in unexpected ways. In our first year in Kenya, Jimmy, the director of the Phoenix, Nairobi's only professional theater, heard that I was an actress. He called and invited me to come downtown and meet him. The Phoenix was one of the few organizations in which Kenyans and expatriates worked together to create professional cultural programs. With a long history of presenting interesting theatrical fare, from Broadway shows to old English drama, the Phoenix was a place with which I was excited about getting involved. When I entered his office, Jimmy, a large Anglo-Kenyan who had been with the theater for over twenty years, handed me a script of *The Gingerbread Lady* by the American playwright Neil Simon.

"What should I read?" I asked, thinking I would do an audition. In his heavy British accent, he nonchalantly mumbled, "It is not necessary to read, you have the part, my dear."

"What part?" I responded, incredulously.

"*You*, without question are Evy, the Gingerbread Lady," Jimmy declared definitively.

Having known me for all of two minutes, without the slightest knowledge of my abilities, Jimmy had given me the lead in a drama in which I played a drunken nymphomaniac on the rebound—not exactly a role that came naturally to me. It required me to be on stage for three straight hours, drinking, swearing, singing, yelling, and crying—the challenge of a lifetime. Maybe I was the only woman crazy enough to take the role.

We rehearsed every night for a month, while Jim, my husband, dutifully played the full-time father at home. I found it incredibly difficult to play the wanton, profligate woman. Each night I would separate from my life as mother and diplomat's wife, dash to the theater, and metamorphose into something, well, utterly different. Jimmy pressed me relentlessly night after night, trying to make me become Evy, the Gingerbread Lady. He would yell, "Slum it more, open your legs when you sit down, talk with less lilt, slur your words!" It was challenging to become the pathetic Evy, who longed to be better, but just couldn't pull herself out of her pathetic misery.

The rehearsals were grueling. I wasn't sure I could pull it off, particularly with Jimmy caustically and obnoxiously daring me to fail. My high-tension relationship with him was exacerbated by the fact that he also played the leading man opposite me. This required me to feel romantic with him on stage—even kissing him madly in one scene—while offstage I found him brutal. Certainly, I was not the first actress to face this kind of dilemma, but it added greatly to the challenge.

The Gingerbread Lady ran for twenty-one nights in a row to diverse Nairobi audiences of Asians, Africans, and Europeans. Some nights Simon's New York–centric jokes fell flat, with few people understanding them. Lines like "He turned his back on me and shoved a Tootsie Roll in his mouth" went right over the heads of many audiences. Few in Kenya know what a Tootsie Roll is, or what a good New York deli is, or the ins and outs of bars in New York City. But despite the cultural gaps, the play was a success for both playgoers and reviewers, who wrote that I played the part with "reckless abandon" — to my mind, a huge compliment.

Jim came to see the show on March 25th, my birthday, which proved the most difficult performance of all. Playing wild, drunken, and lascivious Evy with my husband in row two, took all the concentration I could muster. Later, after the full run of the play, people would whisper and stare at me wherever I went in Nairobi, especially if I had a drink in my hand! Even though my husband had seen me in the show, he never quite understood why I attracted so much attention. The reason, I believe, is that people actually have difficulty separating fiction and reality; to them I was still the drunken nympho Evy.

The Hub of East Africa

Nairobi was similar to and different from Madras. Both cities were once seats of the British Empire, but only in Nairobi do thousands of expatriates continue to reside. Nairobi is, moreover, a hub for development and relief work for the entire East African region. Hundreds of nongovernmental organizations (NGOs) are headquartered in Nairobi. The UN Headquarters for Africa is located on the northern outskirts of Nairobi, and the United Nations Environment Programme (UNEP) has its world headquarters on a huge campus in Nairobi. For Westerners, it is perhaps the most comfortable place to live in East Africa. A few miles south of the equator but at 6,000 feet altitude, it has a wonderfully comfortable climate. No wonder the British stayed in Kenya as long as they could, until the bloody Mau Mau uprising in the 1950s expedited their exit, finally allowing Kenyans their independence in 1963. Jomo Kenyatta, a Kikuyu leader, became Kenya's first president. Today, those who work for CARE, UNICEF, the International Committee of the Red Cross (ICRC), and other aid agencies, as well as business executives and journalists who cover the East Africa region, generally live and work out of Nairobi.

So thoroughly international is Nairobi that it is easy to get sucked into the whirlwind of expatriate life and never get to know Kenyans. The expatriate community is diverse and fascinating, but I was determined I would have some Kenyan friends, just as we previously had Chinese and Indian friends. This proved much harder than I anticipated, however, as colonialism left a deep and indelible mark on East Africa, separating Kenyans from foreigners. Most of my friends in Kenya ended up being foreigners from other countries or white Kenyans of European, primarily English, descent. We had many black Kenyan acquaintances, but sadly, due to the enduring colonial divide, few became our lasting friends, much to my chagrin.

Richard Buckley, our ambassador Prudence Bushnell's husband, made an interesting discovery. While researching the history of their official ambassadorial residence in Nairobi, which had been acquired by the U.S. government in 1945, Dick discovered that the house had been the headquarters for the British war effort in East Africa during World War II and included the office of the notorious Lord Jocelyn Errol. Lord Errol was the extremely dashing leader of the infamous Happy Valley crowd, a wild, irreverent group of English nobility and wealthy foreigners who arrived in the British colony of Kenya in the interwar years and pursued a raucous lifestyle, rife with sex and liquor. A popular saying at the time was, "Are you married, or do you live in Kenya?"

Joss Errol was the Don Juan of the Happy Valley crowd and the most dashingly colorful man in Nairobi at the time. He had affairs with some of the most eligible, and even more of the ineligible, women of British Kenya. Late one evening in 1941, after partying at the exclusive Muthaiga Club with his lover Diana, wife of a prominent English nobleman, Lord Delves Broughton, Lord Errol was murdered, and the tale of "white mischief" became world renowned. The murderer was never determined and the story still lingers, full of mystery, intrigue, and glamour over half a century later.

Dick decided to commemorate his and Pru's house by writing a play about the life and death of Lord Errol. He wrote it as a dinner theater murder mystery, based on James Fox's book, *White Mischief*. Dick asked me to play the American heiress, Alice de Janze. The dark and mysterious, but loose, Alice had been one of the most notorious of the Happy Valley crowd. She had an on-again, off-again affair with Errol. Surely it was just a coincidence, I reassured myself, that I had been cast as a bad girl two years in a row! Playing such intrigue and mystery, however, proved both challenging and fun.

Each performance of the show was completely different, depending on the crowd attending. The performers, in 1940s habiliment and in character, sat scattered among the dinner tables. The audience was tasked with getting into the mindset of 1941 colonial Kenya. The expatriate community in Nairobi and the white Kenyans from the hinterland coffee plantations entered into the drama with great gusto, arriving in full costume—boas, tuxedos, glitter, and plumes. Throughout the evening, we dined and danced. replicating the elegance of the 1940s. About halfway through dinner, the British colonial police arrived, dramatically announcing Lord Errol's murder. They brusquely held the entire room hostage and proceeded to question each of the performers about their whereabouts that night. The chief inspector then charged the dinner guests, based on the events of the evening up to that point, with determining the murderer's identity. The drama was so realistic that performers and dinner guests alike reported they felt they were actually living in the 1940s.

We performed *White Mischief* in many clubs in Kenya—the famed Muthaiga Club itself, where many of the original events took place, the equestrian Karen Club, next to Karen Blixen's (Isak Dinesen) farm, the stunningly elegant Mount Kenya Safari Club, the Lord Errol Restaurant, and the American Club, as well as several elegant private parties. We produced *White Mischief* twelve times during our last two years in Kenya. The actors had a colorful time, while each performance raised money for the charities of the American Women's Club.

At some of the performances, I danced with elderly gentlemen who were contemporaries of the real Alice de Janze. Some actually remembered her and were able to catch me on the facts of her life. "What did you say to your husband when you shot him in Paris, in the Gare du Nord?" one man asked me while we were dancing cheek to cheek. I had great fun improvising my answers, but occasionally some, who were actually there when Alice lived her wild and adventurous life, caught me off guard and completely stumped me with their questions.

At the end of each performance, the dinner guests would cast their ballots for the character they thought was the murderer and explain the rationale for their choice. Oddly enough, whenever the audience voted me the murderer, I reveled in the feeling that my performance had been a true success.

While performing in *White Mischief* I began to meet "White Kenyans," some of whom lived on cattle ranches in the far north, or on the rolling coffee plantations in the foothills of the Aberdare Mountains. Some had lived in Kenya in the 1940s and personally knew the characters we were playing.

Vivacious Petal Allen, had been living in Kenya as a twelve-year-old at the time of the murder. She had been swimming with Lord Errol and Diana on the day of the murder. Petal told us of going with Diana to change after the swim and marveling at Diana's closets full of stunning clothes. She filled us with tales of the people we were playing, describing the personalities of the unique Happy Valley Crowd. Petal's father-in-law by her first marriage had actually been the murder trial prosecutor, and *White Mischief* author James Fox had lived in Petal's family house while researching the book. She knew many specific details about the murder.

Petal herself lived a very romantic Kenyan life. Married to her third husband, hunter–bush pilot and safari guide David Allen, she was the matriarch of a large extended family with many ties to Kenya. She had five children by her first husband and had been in the Hollywood film circuit with her second husband. She seemed to know everyone in Nairobi and introduced me to her friend, Paul Spicer, who had met and was then writing a biography of my character, the alluring Alice de Janze. It was such a thrill to be introduced to his friends at the elegant old Muthaiga Club as the "new Alice." Paul showed me original photos of the gorgeous and mysterious Alice, replete with her boa wrapped around her shoulders—a real boa constrictor—and told tales of her adventures. I wanted to understand this woman more and to be as true to her as I could in my portrayal.

Paul invited us on safari one weekend to Happy Valley to search for Alice's original house, which he had spotted by airplane as he and David Allen scoped out the Rift Valley area. After eight grueling hours driving over dirt roads and across riverbeds, we located the house, tucked in a remote hollow at the foot of the

Aberdare Mountains. Her old house is now a school, but some of the elderly people living in the area actually remembered Alice. One Kikuyu man said his father had been her cook. He said, Alice, an exotic character, had lived alone in the house with her animals, a cheetah and a lion cub, and often rode on horseback over the hills to "Clouds," Lord Errol's sprawling ranch in the next valley. There, she had many rendezvous with him, which could last from several hours to several weeks. Alice also often drove down the Rift Valley into Nairobi. In the 1940s, the drive to Nairobi was a long ordeal, and once people got there, they stayed for weeks on end, partying, cavorting, and bed-swapping. Alice, in the forefront of the Happy Valley Crowd, did plenty of it all. She was even thrown out of Kenya by the proper British colonial authorities for her loose behavior, unbecoming to a single woman.

Through playing Alice in *White Mischief*, I came to meet many other white Kenyans who led lives full of adventure. The older ones knew a Kenya that for them was close to perfect. They flew around Kenya in their private planes from one vast farm to another over the expanses of mountain, savannah, jungle, and desert, viewing vast herds of elephants, wildebeests, giraffe, and zebra, and sometimes dropping in (literally) just for tea, then taking off for the next ranch. These Kenyans have watched as their adopted country has slowly deteriorated in infrastructure, economy, law, and order. They have lived amid the deterioration of the country they love. They are torn between their attachment to this land—its charming people, its climate, beauty and lifestyle—and the realization that it is in rapid decline from overpopulation, poverty, recurrent tribalism, and deteriorating infrastructure. They fear the crime, corruption, and general deterioration of all that they knew. Although Kenya is their home, most are of English descent, and many are beginning to wonder whether they should at long last return to England.

While we lived there, Petal and her family made the decision to return to Bath. Even though Petal's father was the first white man to be declared a Kenyan citizen after independence, her longtime Kenyan family reluctantly closed their family compound, which had been in Nairobi since before Kenyan independence, and moved four generations of Kenyans back to England. The country had grown too corrupt for them, and life had gotten too unsafe.

The same worries bombard rich and poor African Kenyans alike in Nairobi. They, too, fear for their security and wonder what the future holds. Many of those who are able, try to leave or at least send their children abroad for a better future. Many hold dual passports, giving them options for escape. Kenya suffered greatly under the leadership of President Daniel Arap Moi, whose increasingly corrupt government allowed Kenya's infrastructure to deteriorate for more than two decades. Moi left the masses of poor unemployed Kenyans to cope on their own with the scourges of AIDS, poverty, crime, and overpopulation. The poverty and anger among the people has been fertile ground for crime and violence, a violence that has continued to tear apart a once stable country.

Moses and Miracles

Life can be harsh and unfair in Kenya. Moses, our gardener, was a seemingly happy roly-poly man, always helpful, smiling, and pleasant. Under Moses's green thumb, our garden became a wonderful tropical retreat, hidden among newly planted towering banana trees. The climate in Nairobi is perfect for gardens; most days are filled with sun, crisp cool air, and a special clean bright light that comes from the direct equatorial sun. We left our doors and windows wide open, for there are few mosquitoes. We often mused that we were living in paradise. Most days are like the finest spring days in Washington or San Francisco. Flowers and plants grow like wildfire. I loved planning out the drama of the garden with Moses. Jim had the idea of ringing the backyard with fast-growing banana trees to create a private forest glade. Moses found a patch of banana seedlings and planted them. They grew from little sprouts to a lush tropical forest in less than a year. Moses then wove a great arch out of saplings and planted fuchsia-colored bougainvillea to drape over the archway. He planted all of our window boxes with colorful petunias, daisies, and geraniums. A flowering jacaranda tree graced the front entrance to our house, and the backyard had avocado trees so abundantly laden with fruit that we could not keep up with them, and many fell overly ripened to the ground. Everything Moses planted grew into miraculous beauty.

Yet Moses's life was one of intense hardships, always at the edge of survival. He was the father of six children, who remained back in the home province of Kakamega in western Kenya, the land of the Luhya tribe. Kenya is a country of tribes: Kikuyu, Masai, Luo, Luhya, Kalenjin, and many others, each with strong tribal loyalties. Many Kenyans hedge their bets against poverty and disease by having lots of children. Work is difficult to find, except in Nairobi, forcing tens, hundreds of thousands of people to leave their families in their home villages in the countryside and trek to Nairobi in search of jobs. In Nairobi, Moses lived alone in one of countless thousands of tiny, flimsy tin shacks in a vast slum of dark muddy alleys and open sewers called Nairobi Soweto. Just before Moses started working for us, the entire slum burned down, including his little shack, leaving him and thousands of others homeless. He was left with nothing but the clothes on his back. After hiring him, we helped fund the construction of a new house for him in another crowded slum area called Kibera, near the airport,.

One day Moses asked for a few days off to return to his Luhya family in western Kenya, because his little boy was sick. He asked to borrow money to buy medicine for his son. A week later he returned to Nairobi. When, I asked how his son was, he replied, in his quiet, humble, way, "He died, Madam." When I pressed Moses, he explained that his son had had malaria, but unfortunately, Moses had arrived too late with the money to buy medicine. This was the second of his children to die of malaria in this way. His sense of resignation shocked me. I couldn't comprehend his fatal acceptance of this tragedy. But, things like this happen all the time in Kenya, now, more than ever. With the HIV AIDS epidemic, people are dropping like flies. The very people who could make a difference in this country—the doctors, teachers, factory workers, and bankers—are the most at risk. The Moi government paid little attention to this burgeoning epidemic, which was eating at Kenya's very future.

In 2003, four years after we left Kenya, a new opposition government in Kenya began to address this tragic situation. At first, with the newly elected government of Moi Kibaki, Kenyans gained a sense of renewed hope. Many who had left the country returned to contribute to their nation. Corruption, however, is so ingrained in the system that even Kibaki has not been able to escape it. It will take a major miracle to undo the damage of corruption and tribal rivalry and rebuild the nation.

Evolution and Creation

Since my business, Global Adjustments, was doing so well in Madras, India, I had hoped to set up a branch office in Kenya, where there was no relocation company of its kind. Western business and other foreigners need help adjusting to Nairobi, especially if they have never before lived in Africa or the Third World. They may not be used to dodging potholes, the lack of law and order, rising crime, the prevalence of disease, hiring household staff, bartering for goods, or the failing telephone system—just for starters! A person transferring from United Nations Geneva to United Nations Nairobi, for example, would likely be shocked at the difference in living standards, sanitation, sense of time, ethnic and tribal divisions, and customs encountered. Coming from nations where everything works like clockwork to Africa, where things are haphazard and unpredictable, can be disconcerting and overwhelming; but with help, I believed, living in Kenya could be the adventure of a lifetime. I intended to provide that help. So, I asked two Dutch women to be my partners, and we opened a consulting branch of Global Adjustments in Nairobi. Our company slogan in Kenya was "Into Africa," as opposed to Karen Blixen's "Out of Africa."

We worked to interest international businesses and the U.N. in hiring us to help relocate their employees to Kenya. We quickly learned that Nairobi, in contrast to Madras, is not an expanding market. Rather, those expatriates, who do move to Nairobi, are normally just replacing their predecessors, and thus inherit their houses, servants, and schools. The arriving employee moves directly into his predecessor's setup, often a walled estate that protects the family from the rawness of Nairobi streets. Thus, there is much less demand in Kenya than in India for a relocation firm to take care of these needs.

Newly arrived expatriates are introduced to the international community by their predecessors and generally ushered into the comfortable and privileged expatriate world of golf, teas, club life, and going on safari. Consequently, our client potential proved quite small. Perhaps if the government in Kenya had made conditions more attractive for international business, there might have been a better market for the relocation business. But with the economic doldrums and rampant corruption, new businesses were not moving into Nairobi in 1997. On the contrary, foreign businesses were beginning to move employees out of a Kenya in serious decline.

Because Global Adjustments was not proving a success in Kenya, I began to devote my time to the National Museum of Kenya. One of Kenya's claims to fame, thanks to the work of the Leakey family, is its recognition of Africa as the cradle of the human race. Paleontologists Louis Leakey and his wife Mary Leakey spent their lives searching for and finding paleontological clues to the origins of mankind. The National Geographic Society has sponsored the family's explorations for years. The Leakeys' early work at Olduvai Gorge in Tanzania uncovered some of the earliest human fossils of the manlike creatures called *australopithecines*. Following in their footsteps, their son, Richard Leakey, continued the family's major finds, including the bones of *homo erectus*, "Turkana Boy," and skeletal parts that reinforce the argument that the first humans emerged in Africa.

Much of their research and many of their actual finds are housed in the National Museum of Kenya in Nairobi. While studying to become a docent at the museum, I was taught by Richard Leakey's wife, Maeve, who along with her daughter, now leads some of the newest efforts in the field. She taught us the history of the Leakey family's work and her most recent finds, which date the earliest humans in East Africa to as long ago as 4.2 million years. Many of the fossilized bones are housed in a huge vault in the National Museum. Walking through the vault takes one past the strange bones of hominids and animals that have long since become extinct. While on safari digs, walking on the floor of the vast Rift valley, looking for bones gave me a sense of the central importance of Africa as a place whence we human beings evolved and became civilized. It was amazing to live in Kenya and think of these hominid creatures walking around that part of Africa so long ago. Working and learning in this fertile environment was thrilling and greatly enriched my experience of Kenya.

Learning that the earliest humans emerged in Kenya reinforced my feeling that Kenya may have been the locale of the original Garden of Eden. The great diversity of animal life in Kenya, with its stunning array of colors, designs, size, agility, and beauty, testifies to God's majesty. Our visits to the Masai Mara, Amboselli, Tsavo, and Samburu game parks filled me with awe and reverence at this incredible creation.

We took every opportunity to go on safari and experience Kenya's remarkable natural treasures. Nothing matches the vast expanse of land strewn with animals of every size, color and shape, the wide skies with clear bright light, and the near perfect climate. Our family spent many days driving in four-wheel-drive vehicles searching for wild animals. Christopher and Caroline loved bouncing around the vast savannah spotting gazelles, giraffes, lions, cheetah, and hippos. We spent hot dry days on safari, then we gathered around campfires in the cool nights to share our tales of the day. I sometimes played guitar and sang with my kids for visitors from around the globe who gathered nightly around the fires. The memories of these safaris are viscerally sealed in our hearts. The sad reality, however, is that Kenya's burgeoning population and urban growth is slowly destroying much of this paradise.

Working at the museum as a guide, I sometimes discussed with visitors the theories of evolution and creation. Proof of both exists side by side in Kenya. While the creation is magnificent, the idea of evolution is also remarkably visible. One of the big questions asked by paleontologists is: What is the definition of a human being and when did human beings emerge as a distinct species? To many paleontologists, bipedalism, or the ability to walk on two feet, defines the beginning of mankind. But Richard Leakey spoke to us one day and argued that perhaps the display of compassion was the defining factor. He conjectured that the moment an early hominid asked his fellow hominid, "Can I help you?" civilization as we know it may have begun.

Leakey went on to tell us an amazing tale about modern-day lack of compassion. He lost both of his legs in an airplane accident, one many Kenyans believe may not have been an accident but a plot to stop his outspoken criticism of the corrupt and authoritarian Moi government. Richard told us about one day when he was in London as the guest of honor at a large gathering of paleontologists. Walking across the street in the rain, he slipped and fell breaking his prosthetics. Unable to raise himself, he had to roll around on the ground and crawl across the street on his stumps amid morning traffic. Drivers yelled obscenities at him from their car windows. "Get out of the street you drunken bum!" He was forced to crawl back to his hotel on the ground in the pouring rain. Noting that no one helped him, he said, "I am not certain that civilization has brought increased compassion from one person to another, even after thousands of years."

Richard's father, Louis Leakey, was the mentor of many well-known researchers in East Africa, including Jane Goodall, who has done significant work with chimpanzees and is a world renowned promoter of the environment, and Diane Fosse, who was murdered while working with gorillas in Rwanda. We visited Goodall's chimp preserve near the Sweetwater Game Reserve that bestrides the equator in central Kenya. At Sweetwater, Jim and I and the kids lived in tents that opened directly on the game preserve, where throughout the night and day animals came very close to drink from the salt lick. It was magical to see gazelles, giraffe, and zebras so close by. Face to face with Jane Goodall's chimpanzees, I could not help but reflect on our human race and examine the progress we have made as we diverged from these apes. It is remarkably sad that we humans can still behave so primitively toward one another, with such a lack of compassion. But I pray that Jane Goodall was right when she named her recent book *Reason for Hope*.

Another thing that amazed and fascinated me was the vast number of bird species in East Africa. At the museum's Ornithology Department, I discovered that over 500 different species of birds can be found in Nairobi alone. Christopher and I used to wake up before dawn and tiptoe out onto the balcony of his room. There we would identify dozens of varieties of birds right in our own garden. On any given morning, we would see Hadada Ibis, hornbills, sunbirds, weaverbirds, eagles, kites, and many more species right from our own balcony. How delightful those early morning sessions were, with Christopher and I wrapped in our blankets spotting birds as the sun came up. When the birds dispersed at sunrise, we would go in for breakfast and chatter excitedly about the birds we had identified. The sun is like clockwork on the equator, rising almost exactly at 6 a.m. and setting at 6 p.m., making the transition from light to darkness just a matter of minutes and omitting the long drawn-out, but often beautiful, sunrises and sunsets we know in North America.

Terror Strikes

In stark contrast to the glorious countryside of Kenya, the city of Nairobi epitomizes where humankind has gone wrong. Each time you venture out in Nairobi, especially at night, you play Russian roulette. Carjackings, robberies, and even student riots are a part of everyday life. While we lived in Nairobi, some of my good friends were carjacked at gunpoint, thrown into their car trunks, dumped out at some remote location unknown to them, and left to find their way home. They were the lucky ones, however. A teacher at the International School of Kenya was killed because she refused to give up her car. Another friend, whose husband was with Coca-Cola in Nairobi, had robbers climb in through her window at night, hold a gun to her twelve-year-old son's head, take all of their valuables, throw her into a car, and abduct her. After hours of driving around in the dark in her nightgown, she was released far out in the bush. Entering his house gate, a German diplomat was followed and killed. An Indian family of six, asleep in their house, was murdered. And on and on it goes. You can never be sure whether something similar might happen to you, and it could happen anywhere and anytime. Although it sounds impossibly gruesome, you learn to live with your antennae up. In Nairobi, there is a constant uneasiness, and yet, one has to get on with life. You can either hide, paralyzed with fear, or accept it and go out. We chose to live fully, to socialize and enjoy life, despite the risks, but always with a sense of the real danger involved.

One of the risks that I most disliked, however, was taking Christopher and Caroline to the American Embassy to see the doctor. Located in an unsafe part of downtown Nairobi, it seemed odd that we were expected to take our small children to the Embassy to see the doctor. Each time I took them there, I felt I was taking a risk. I expressed my concerns to Ambassador Prudence Bushnell on several occasions in writing. In response, Pru called a town meeting in which the community discussed moving the medical unit to a safer location. I found myself in the middle of a hot debate, representing the unofficial side of the equation—those who wanted the unit moved. However, many embassy employees strongly opposed the idea as too inconvenient for them, so the medical unit remained in the Embassy in downtown Nairobi.

As a political officer, Jim was responsible for covering the many opposition parties. During the run-up to the elections, large-scale demonstrations by the opposition parties often turned violent. One night in late May, Jim and I drove downtown for our wedding anniversary dinner. As we turned off Harambee Avenue toward the historic Norfolk Hotel, a sea of angry students from Nairobi University suddenly enveloped us. The rioting students threw huge rocks at our car. Slumped down on the floor of our car, I radioed the embassy for escape routes. With the instructions from the Marine guards at the Embassy, Jim drove wildly, scurrying down back roads to escape the hurling rocks and violence.

Despite the city's volatility, we nevertheless had to drive to the most dangerous section to get to the Embassy for medical and other administrative needs. I once again wrote to the ambassador suggesting a new location for the medical unit would be advisable during this turmoil. Ambassador Bushnell fully realized that the location of the Embassy was not secure for Americans. She had written to the State Department several times, including a letter directly to Secretary Madeleine Albright, requesting enhanced security. Her numerous pleas went unheeded, because Nairobi was not considered a "high threat" post to those at the State Department.

On the morning of August 7, 1998, I had yet again to take my children to the Embassy medical unit for their school physicals. We had just returned to Kenya from home leave in the United States and England, and school was about to start. Reluctantly, I drove to the Embassy with Christopher and Caroline, parked by the rear gate, chatted a bit with the friendly guard, entered the Embassy's rear basement entrance, and went down the hall to the doctor's office. In the medical unit, I realized I had left the children's school medical forms at home. The nurse suggested, "If you go home and hurry back before 10:30, the doctor will still have time to see your children." I raced home to get the forms. While I was in the house, the children hid our cocker spaniel, Jingles, in the back seat of the car, and we started off toward the Embassy again. After discovering the dog in the back seat, I admonished them, "We can't bring Jingles to the Embassy! Dogs aren't allowed in embassies you silly guys." This distraction made us a bit late. We arrived back at the Embassy at about 10:33—I was watching the time closely, because we were already beyond 10:30, a tardiness that would prove providential. We were supposed to meet Jim upstairs on the first floor to take a photo for Caroline's passport, cash a check, and then have lunch. We had dressed up because we were meeting Jim—Caroline in a little red dress and sandals, Christopher in his blue blazer, and I in a snazzy pink sheath and blue blazer. They were excited to be meeting Daddy at work.

I hurriedly parked in the Embassy's rear parking lot, next to a delivery truck that had not been there before. We walked in front of the truck and to the gate and asked the embassy guard to let us in. He seemed hesitant and nervous, which seemed odd, since just a few minutes earlier he had been relaxed and playful with Christopher and Caroline. Now, however, he seemed distracted and distant. There I stood with my two small children asking that he open that gate, which he clearly didn't want to do. He finally reluctantly opened the gate, and we hurried down the garage ramp, through the basement door, and down the long corridor to the Embassy medical unit. Caroline and Christopher settled on the floor, to build Lego towers, and I breathlessly handed in the school medical forms. Moments later, at precisely 10:34 a.m., a loud boom pierced the air, and I turned to the nurse and said, "That sounds like a bomb."

She said, "It's Nairobi, you know, probably a bus backfiring." Seconds later, a second much larger explosion shattered the air, and the entire world went dark while the earth shook. I was thrown to the floor in darkness. Completely stunned, it took me a moment to realize what had happened.

This was what a bomb felt like. A bomb *had* hit the Embassy. I called desperately in the darkness, "Caroline, Christopher, Are you all right? Where are you!?"

Caroline cried out, "Is this a nuclear bomb, Mommy?"

"No, it is not a nuclear bomb, but it is a bomb, and you must do exactly as I say. We are going to get out of here, you both must stay very close and follow me."

We grabbed for each other and held tightly, huddling on the floor in the rubble. I held five-year-old Caroline's hand, and she held onto eight-year-old Christopher. I, instinctively, felt in the darkness for my purse and actually found it. Then slowly and silently, we groped our way through the rubble and the pitch dark to where I thought the door had been. The mental floor plan of the basement hall in my mind was all I had to go by. I led Christopher and Caroline with one hand, and stretched the other out in front of me feeling in the dark, fearful that I might touch an electric wire or worse. The acrid dust-laden air was hard to breathe, and we had to crouch down low and almost crawl over glass to get below the cement dust and debris filling the air. Caroline and Christopher did not cry but solemnly held my hand tight and followed me.

Adrenaline made me move fast and determinedly. In the darkness of the hallway, I stumbled over a woman lying injured on the floor. We assured her the doctor was following right behind us. In the inky darkness, we could hear voices calling "Where is the door?" I just kept following my mental map, feeling my way down the long basement hallway, groping where I thought a door must be, through rubble and cement.

Finally, I saw a small beam of light coming from a hole in the wall. We climbed through this hole into the basement garage. Voices in the distance cried out in agony. I saw a bright orange light and pulled the children up the garage ramp. We ran out into a wall of flames. Where our car had been parked was the epicenter of the explosion. The car was obliterated. The rubble of buildings surrounded a huge hole in the ground. The 34-story Cooperative Bank building behind the Embassy was blasted through and tilting, with people blackened with soot stumbling out the doors. Another building had completely pancake-collapsed to the rear of the Embassy.

We ran around the building, stuck inside the perimeter steel fencing. The moment we rounded the corner, miraculously, there was Jim clinging to the steel fence at the front of the Embassy. The children shrieked "Daddy, Daddy!" Caroline slipped through the fence into his arms. Somebody hoisted Christopher over the fence. Blocked by the steel bars, my body shook and trembled, as Jim and another officer, Kevin Richardson, pried apart the steel fence with their bare hands and yanked me through. A man stood stripped naked and bleeding screaming behind me. I reached for Jim.

He had presumed we were dead, thinking that we'd been on the first floor of the Embassy waiting for him. As he stumbled and slid down the shattered stairwell from the fourth floor, stumbling over rubble and people, he saw only death and destruction on each lower floor. Everyone on the first floor, where we were supposed to have been, was dead. But, somehow miraculously united, we stood there outside the Embassy trembling and crying with relief.

Fearing what might happen next, we ran down the street away from the building. Friends I saw standing in shock I urged to come with us. We ran against a sea of people converging on the Embassy. All was chaos. I thought to myself, this is what hell must be like. Rumors were flying. People were saying that the U.S. Embassies in Tanzania, Uganda, Ethiopia, and Sudan had all been simultaneously bombed. I wasn't sure where the terrorists were. We kept running. Jim spotted a car with embassy license plates on the other side of the road. We leapt the meridian and Jim shoved us into the van, slammed the door, told the driver to take us home, then ran back to the smoking Embassy to help others.

It was only then that Caroline and Christopher became afraid, thinking that their father might die. I tried to tell them that Daddy would be all right, but I had no idea what was happening or where the terrorists might strike next. I noticed a cut on Caroline's leg and blood dribbling down from it. Miraculously that was our only injury. We, a family of four, had somehow all survived the bombing. The driver drove on the wrong side of the road, on the sidewalks, and through the center of circles to get us out of the city. When he dropped us at a point as far as he could go, we ran the rest of the way home through the streets—Caroline's little red dress black with soot, my face and hair white with cement, and my pink dress blackened, our ears full of cement. We looked half crazed. As we entered our compound, the guards and staff were shocked and fearful. I threw away my cement-encrusted purse and shoes. We went into our house, closed the door, and bathed the bomb off our bodies, the cement out of our eyes and ears, and calmed our nerves and breathed.

My main objective became instantly clear: get things as normal and safe for our children as possible. Caroline and Christopher, and I had lunch together, played on the playground, and watched videotapes of the *Brady Bunch*, whose simple happiness soothed them. Meanwhile, the whole world outside seemed to be going crazy. I could hear voices flying back and forth over our embassy radio system; things were in total crisis, everyone trying to help restore some order. My friend Dick Buckley, the ambassador's husband, not knowing the children and I had been in the bomb, called and gave me a list of twenty-five things to do to help the victims. I accepted the tasks and got to work, setting up a blood bank, making sandwiches for emergency volunteers, and organizing meals for grieving families.

Jim didn't come back home until late that night. He expected to find us packed to leave, waiting on the curb. When he arrived home at around midnight, he couldn't believe we were all right. He told me the tragic news of friends who had been killed or injured. My good friend, Sue Bartley, had lost her son, Jay, and they feared also her husband, Julian. Michelle, a mother of three was dead. Louise, the spouse of a Center for Disease Control officer, scout leader, veterinarian, and a good friend of mine, was dead. The foreign national in Jim's office, an embassy driver, and several embassy colleagues were dead. It was impossible to take in. Over 250 people, mostly Kenyans, were killed in the bombing. I was overwhelmed; tears would not stop flowing down my face. The shock I felt, and the constant playing out of "what if" scenarios over and over in my mind, left me completely raw.

The days that followed brought us anxiety and deep sorrow. We received letters, calls, and e-mails from hundreds of supportive friends. Calls from all over the world came at all hours of the day and night. My parents, friends, and family all offered their support. Within hours of the bombing, Ranjini called from India. My brother

Bobby offered to come to Kenya. Chrissie, my sister, checked with me hourly. These calls of support meant so much to me during those days of sadness.

Although many people were killed, our embassy community rallied and began to pull itself back together. Jim and I considered whether to leave Nairobi and go back to the United States—all embassy families were offered the option of curtailing their assignment and leaving post. Surprisingly enough, however, only one family chose to leave. Instead, we all started to help in the relief effort.

Post-Traumatic Stress

The whole city and the entire country shared the bomb tragedy and responded to the crisis by reaching out and supporting one another. One month before the bombing, I had become chair of the American Women's Association (AWA), a large international social service organization in Nairobi. From this platform, I was able to act on behalf of the Nairobi American community. Within twenty-four hours of the bombing, we ran a full-page statement in the main newspaper, *The Nation*, expressing America's sympathy for and solidarity with the Kenyan victims.

The AWA set up a Bomb Relief Fund to help Kenyan blast victims. As AWA chair, I went on television and in the newspapers soliciting funds. We offered our blood bank to victims and organized ongoing meals for victims' families.

Jim and his fellow Foreign Service officers and those Kenyan employees who survived determined that the terrorists would not win and quickly restarted embassy operations. Under the leadership of Ambassador Prudence Bushnell, everyone worked tirelessly, despite his or her sorrows and fears. They worked to clear the destroyed Embassy building. The embassy offices were moved temporarily to the offices of the U.S. Agency for International Development (USAID), doubling the staff in what were already cramped quarters. The ten-story USAID building was surrounded with armed Marine guards, rows of sandbags and barbed wire, and perimeter roadblocks. Into this war zone, Jim went to work each day. Neither I nor the children ever again went back into the Embassy in Nairobi.

We attended many memorial services over the first few weeks. Poignant moments were shared, and Ambassador Bushnell lent her courageous words of encouragement to all of us who were suffering in the community. Secretary of State Madeleine Albright flew out to Kenya to show us her support. She was greeted with heavy hearts. She arrived late at night, after we had been waiting for many hours to see her. She shook hands with each of the family members who had lost a loved one and presented all of us with a plaque of honor, which seemed like a rather trivial recompense after the incredible trauma we had all suffered. Her distraction may have been warranted, because that very night she and President Clinton decided that, in retaliation, our country would launch attacks on the Sudan and on Osama Bin Laden's camps in Afghanistan.

In Nairobi, we lived in fear of another attack. I never knew who I was passing on the street, whether they were Sudanese Muslim terrorists or Kenyans who had lost a family member for which they blamed and hated Americans. It was an extremely difficult time. To reduce the feeling of living exposed and targeted, I removed the diplomatic license plates from our car, which identified us as Americans, and from then on drove around with a lower profile and no plates. Amazingly, I continued to drive around Nairobi and Kenya for the following year without any license plates, and no one ever stopped my car.

In retrospect, it was an extremely important decision for us to stay in Kenya. The children were able to go back to the International School of Kenya and to their friends just a few days after the bombing. The entire school community proved incredibly supportive. Beyond our immediate community, the whole of Kenya had been directly or indirectly affected by the bombing, making this tragedy an experience shared by all around us. Had we gone back to America, where the bombing quickly became ancient history and people did not understand what we had been through, it would have been much more difficult to come to terms with the trauma of the bombing. Actively responding and just talking about the events proved to be very healing.

The children and Jim and I told our stories again and again for the FBI and the news media that flooded into Nairobi. The media descended on our house immediately after the bomb. Perhaps that was because the story of our family may have been the only positive one among so much sadness, or because we seemed like any typical American family, but one that had been caught in the crossfire of international terrorism. BBC News, NBC News, ABC News, and the *New York Times* interviewed us. Ted Koppel did a half-hour program on the bombing on *Nightline* that centered on our family. My heart ached watching little Christopher and Caroline interviewed about bombs and terrorists. The children were articulate and brave in retelling their experience, despite some media insensitivity. One reporter from *Good Morning America* asked 8-year-old Christopher, "So are you really afraid now?" With my motherly protectiveness, I almost cut into the live program to chastise the reporter for his insensitivity.

One day, a seven-member FBI team came to our house and interviewed the children about what they had seen that day, focusing in particular on the strange truck we parked beside just before the bomb went off. Christopher tried to answer their questions, stating that he couldn't remember what the people in the truck looked like. Christopher later wrote his own version of his experiences of that morning in a book, which he illustrated and sent to President Clinton, describing the events of the bombing and asking the president to stop the terrorists from any more violence. In his letter he pleaded, "Please President Clinton, do something to stop those people who want to hurt Americans." All of this talking actually proved therapeutic for our family. Over the following year, we talked about our memories and fears again and again until we were able to begin letting them go—although one never truly ever can forget such tragic events.

Focusing on the American Women's Association Bomb Relief Fund also helped me a great deal. Diving into this work, I was able to respond positively to the sadness and horror of the bombing. We raised funds by doing small benefit events in Nairobi. Tapping both the international school network and the AWA network, I was able to solicit funds internationally. Donations and letters poured in from around the world.

With the help of USAID, AWA located several Kenyan children who had been blinded or visually impaired by the blast. Their school bus had been circling the roundabout in front of the Embassy when the bomb exploded. Luckily, a car sat between their bus and the Embassy, so none of the children had been killed, but flying glass imbedded in their eyes blinded several children. They were Asian Kenyans, Kenyans of Indian decent who were part of a tight Indian community. When I first met with them, the children seemed stunned and confused. They couldn't see who was talking to them, so I took their hands in mine. I explained that I was an American who had also been in the bomb blast with my children and that I wanted to help them. With the support that came pouring in, we were able to send some of the children to the United States for corrective eye surgery. Boston Eye and Ear Infirmary generously offered to perform the surgery for free, and we located free housing in Boston. In the end so much in-kind support was offered that we didn't need to use the AWA's relief funds for the eye surgery. That left us free to help other victims.

Several months after the bombing, we located Teresa Njenga Karanja, a woman who had been paralyzed by the bomb. She had been working in the thirty-six-story Cooperative Bank building directly behind the Embassy when the blast hit. Unfortunately a wall fell on her, trapping her and leaving her unable to move. Hours later, she woke up in Mater Hospital, a small hospital on the outskirts of Nairobi. It took several days for her family to find her, having searched all the major hospitals and the morgues. Her husband, Njenga, is a resilient man, full of energy. It was he who found us and led us to her. When I first met Teresa Karanja, she had been lying in her hospital bed for almost four months, continually praying to God to help her. The doctors in the hospital did not have the resources and training to help a victim with a spinal cord injury. Her husband realized he had to act quickly or she might never be able to leave the hospital. When I went to visit her in her bed, she was lying flat on her back, teary-eyed most of the time. She kept repeating, as she read the Bible, "Please God help me," but it was clear her muscles had atrophied for four months, leaving her much weaker than when she had arrived.

After I made a presentation about Teresa to the AWA, the Board of Directors voted to fund her rehabilitation for several months in a modern hospital facility in South Africa. AWA donated US$10,000 to cover Teresa's rehabilitation, and air transport for her and her husband to and from South Africa. When I went to see her the second time, to tell her that AWA would fund her trip, her four children were there with her. Fortunately, since it was already December, I had brought Christmas gifts for each of them—toys from America. Her middle son, twelve-year-old Charles, was sullen and angry. His father told me he was angry with Americans for being the cause of this trauma to his mother. I sat down to talk with him explaining that my children and I were also in the bombing, and although we weren't physically hurt, we were emotionally traumatized. I wanted him to know that we understood how bad he felt and how sad we were for his mother and his family. He was surprised to learn that the bomb had injured Americans, too. With our help, Teresa and her husband left for South Africa just before Christmas. That was the first time she had been out of her bed in four months, since the day the bomb hit.

The Kenyan press began to manifest signs of anti-Americanism, blaming the United States for the bombing. It was particularly painful to read such criticism when we all were victims, Kenyans and Americans alike. Rather than reporting the American tragedies, some of the news media made the United States the scapegoat, portraying our country as responsible for the trauma. Richard Leakey, the famed white Kenyan anthropologist who had been supported by National Geographic for decades, wrote a very anti-American editorial in the press. Having met him at the National Museum, I telephoned him and told him there was no room for this hostility when there were so many injured people on all sides. I was angry that this criticism came from the very man who had talked so eloquently about compassion. He backed down; and when he came to the AWA as a guest speaker later that month, he left politics out of his comments. There was a tremendous failure on the part of U.S. public diplomacy, which failed to respond adequately to the enormous anti-American sentiment in the Kenyan press. Conversations like mine with Teresa's young son, Charles, and with Richard Leakey, were the only effective channels for letting Kenyans know that Americans suffered greatly too, otherwise they would never have learned this from their press.

During her three months in South Africa, Teresa's family sent us notes describing her steady progress. She learned to transfer herself into and out of a wheelchair, as well as in and out of a swimming pool where she swam daily. She learned to dress herself, move her hips and with calipers to even stand and try to walk. Meeting other people with spinal cord injuries, she felt encouraged and empowered. This was remarkably good news, considering the condition in which Teresa had left Kenya. We were hopeful and read the news with tears in our eyes.

At the end of March 1999, Teresa returned home from South Africa. Jim and I went to the airport to greet her. There were approximately a hundred family and friends there to meet her. With a special airport pass from the embassy, Jim and I were able to go out onto the runway to meet her when she got off the plane. When she emerged from the airplane, she was dressed gloriously in a red suit and a big red hat. Smiling broadly, she gave us two-thumbs-up from atop the stairway of the plane. I had never felt happier at any moment in my life. Enthusiastically, she told us stories of all that she did in South Africa and of the friends she had made there. The greatest rehabilitation, she insisted, was that of her husband, Njenga, a Kenyan man who had learned that it was all right for a man to help his wife. He agreed that he, too, had changed dramatically. Right there in the airport, she struggled to demonstrate how she could stand with the calipers.

Teresa's story was carried on the front pages of Kenya's newspapers the next day. Though she returned in a wheelchair, she was clearly a changed woman. Full of hope and enthusiasm for life, she intended to go back to work and to again do many of the things she had done before the bomb. Jim and I embraced her and her family that night. Pleased that AWA had funded her rehabilitation, I was glad that we, as Americans, were able to help Kenyan victims like Teresa. Clearly our intervention made a big impact in her life. She was able to go home for the first time since the bombing. Had she stayed in Kenya, she might never have left the hospital.

Realizing that life was not going to be easy for Teresa, about a week later, I visited her at her home in East Nairobi. She lived in a small cement row house in a lower middle class suburb of Nairobi.

It was clear that life in a wheelchair was going to be tough. The roads were Swiss cheese–potholed, where existent at all; house floors were uneven and the toilet was in a room not big enough for a wheelchair to enter. The stove was too high for her to reach from the wheelchair. She and her husband were brimming with confidence, however, that everything would work out. The AWA decided to give her a bit more money to renovate her house for wheelchair accessibility. The press again interviewed her and continued to tell her story in the papers. Once again, she made a valiant effort to stand up with calipers for the press, but I knew in my heart she would remain in her wheelchair for the rest of her life. The big question was whether her Kenyan husband would indeed continue to stand by her side.

About a month later, Njenga and Teresa invited the Huskey family out to their family farm on the edge of the Great Rift Valley. All four of us drove out to celebrate Teresa's daughter Rose's birthday. We met Teresa's in-laws, saw the chickens, pigs, and cows, and tromped around the small farm. I brought a chocolate birthday cake. When the music played, it seemed as if my whole life's training had led to this one moment when I taught Teresa how to dance in her wheelchair. Over the years I had trained people all over the world in wheelchair dance through my work with Very Special Arts International, but this was deeply personal. There I was dancing with Teresa, who had survived the same bomb that I had, dancing with her on her Kenyan farm, because she *had* to know that life was going to be all right. It took everything I had to hold back the tears.

With the remaining money in the relief fund, we paid for the rehabilitation of a man who had lost his hearing. He had five children to feed but was unable to work after the bombing because he was deaf. We funded an operation to insert a small microphone into his ear canal to allow him to hear and, we all hoped, get back to work. We also supported the counseling of several people who had lost their businesses and needed finances to begin again.

As I met with each of them and discussed their losses, I grew to realize the full horror of the Embassy bombing, which had a ripple of disastrous effects on many people's lives across Kenya. One woman, working on a nearby street corner when the bomb hit, was trampled underfoot by hundreds of people running from the site. Her shop was destroyed and her eyesight impaired by the head injuries she received. A man we met had his head scarred and distorted and his eyesight was almost gone. He had been a taxi driver and wanted to return to work, but didn't know how to begin again. We set up counselors for them and gave them the remainder of our relief fund, realizing all the while that no amount of money would ever be enough to heal them. In all, we provided about US$20,000 in bomb relief aid, while USAID provided millions, all of which went quite a long way in Kenya but could never repair the hearts and the psyches of the Kenyan people.

In the months after the bombing, it was difficult to interact with my friends who were still focused on playing golf and bridge or going horseback riding. Living far from the blast, many of my expatriate friends had barely been touched by the bombing. All the while, I was meeting people daily whose lives were shattered and forever altered, either by physical impairment or by personal loss.

Sue Bartley, a dear friend, lost both her husband, Julian, our consul general, and her son, Jay, who had been working in the Embassy as a summer intern. The sorrow was unfathomable, as I helped her clean out her house and pack up both her husband's belongings and her son's room. It was one of the hardest things we all had ever lived through. While cataloguing Julian's extensive jazz collection and noting each jazz recording, I felt as if I could understand him better. He was a man who had been full of life, a gregarious, big-hearted man who loved music and dance and had served his country well for most of his adult life. Now he was gone, and he took his son Jay, who was only nineteen years old, along with him.

Sue asked me to play the piano at the memorial service for her family in Nairobi. Not sure whether I would be able to play at such an emotional event and in front of so many people, so many who had been through unbearable suffering, I was extremely emotional. It was the first time that most of the victims of the bombing had gathered together. I was afraid I would burst into tears and not be able to function. Ambassador Bushnell and her husband Dick were in the front row, behind them hundreds of people who struggled under a shroud of sadness. Fingers trembling, I pulled myself together and played and sang "Amazing Grace," while the hundreds of still shell-shocked people sang together. Although it was deeply stressful, I did this for my friend Sue. It was important for me to share with all the victims in their sorrow. In turn, this actually helped me deal with my own trauma and express my profound sadness.

After cleaning out her house for five days, I accompanied Sue to the airport and put her on a plane headed back to the United States, with the bodies of her family in the cargo hold. They were leaving after thirty years of service to our country in the State Department, two of them in body bags, with Sue hoping to make sense out of their lives.

Giving Back to Kenya

In the year following the bombing, I was able to make some further contributions to Kenya's recovery and development as chair of the AWA. We raised more funds to build a health clinic run by women in a remote rural district in Machakos. With a group of AWA members, I drove to Machakos for the clinic's grand opening. It took almost eight hours driving over barely discernible roads, through some of the driest terrain I have ever seen. There did not seem to be a drop of water in the entire region. We crossed riverbeds that were stone dry, through mile after mile of sagebrush, without any edible vegetation. Yet, when we arrived, there stood the new clinic, built wholly by the women of the village with AWA funds. Three hundred villagers were lined up, ready to enter the clinic as soon as we inaugurated it. The women in this abysmally poor area of Machakos had, with our funds, made their own bricks and constructed this four-room clinic, complete with a laboratory. AWA also funded the medical supplies, beds, windows, and lights. It was humbling to see what our limited funds were able to produce.

During the rest of that year, AWA held several fundraisers to support other development projects. We hosted a golf tournament, a classical quartet concert, and a huge Christmas bazaar. The funds we raised were earmarked for construction of a school in another extremely poor area of Kenya that had been devastated by the El Niño floods.

As the end of the millennium approached, several of us had the idea of staging a review of the best American music of the twentieth century. After the bombing, we realized that the international community of Nairobi needed an uplifting event to take our minds off the harsh experiences and the deep sadness. We pulled together a cast of singers, dancers, and musicians for a musical show we called, "Red, Hot and Blue." We studied and discussed the great musical contributions of the United States and how to do the songs and dances and portray the feeling of each decade. Just deciding on a selection of songs from the vast array of music Americana in the twentieth century was a challenge. We selected songs such as, "Charleston," "Chattanooga Choo Choo," "Rock around the Clock Tonight," and "Aquarius" from *Hair*. The cast was a group of highly versatile and talented people. Steve, our musical director/ keyboardist, and Bobby, our guitarist, could play almost any genre of music by ear. Our Kenyan bass guitarist had never heard most of the American music before, but picked up the bass rhythms rapidly. Our group of singers was incredibly talented—a Danish opera singer who pulled off Diana Ross and the Everly Brothers with amazing skill; a Dutch singer who had sung with the Tommy Dorsey Band throughout Europe; and Eileen, an American country western singer, who could belt out one mean gospel song.

One dancer was a French mime and actor who could jitterbug better than most Americans. Another dancer, John Allen, a white Kenyan pilot, discovered that dancing and performing on stage was a "better rush" than skydiving. We choreographed dances from the 1920s, '30s, '40s, '50s, '60s, '70s, and '80s. John Allen's wife, Annaliza, and I danced the '20s Charleston, the '30s swing, the '50s jitterbug, and the free-form movements of the '60s and '70s, while the musicians rocked.

Because people in Nairobi were desperate to get on with their lives, we had a number of bookings even before opening night. We were invited to perform at the prestigious Muthaiga Club, the Karen Club next to the Karen Blixen plantation, at a restaurant named after the infamous Lord Errol, at the American Club, the Carnivore Club, and the International School of Kenya (ISK). After a number of long rehearsals, the show opened at the Muthaiga Club, the centerpiece of British Kenya. We toured for several months, performing to enthusiastic appreciative audiences. Each unique setting proved to house an extremely different audience to be won over. We designated each performance a benefit to raise funds to build schools in a rural part of Kenya. Our Nairobi audiences, starved for evenings of joy and uplifting music, went wild with enthusiasm. Even the people at the staid old Muthaiga Club loved the show; the members were dancing in the aisles, singing along with us at every show and calling for encores long into the night.

To my great surprise, Teresa Karanja and her husband came to one of the shows at the Carnivore Restaurant. After the show, Teresa, in a red baseball cap and red bomber jacket, rolled her wheelchair into the Carnivore disco, and she and I danced along with the Nairobi night people. It was an amazing encore to this traumatic year.

We held our last show at Christopher and Caroline's school, the International School of Kenya (ISK). The performance was a benefit to raise funds for a new performing arts center at ISK. With over three hundred fifty people in the audience, including Jim and the children, their teachers, Rose, our cook, and Nancy, our babysitter, it was a wonderful way to say good-bye to Kenya and to leave a concrete legacy of our memorable, poignant, and tragic years there.

Living in Kenya, one would be foolish to miss the amazing opportunities for travel. During our years in Kenya, we took many fantastic holidays to the Swahili coast and to Kenya's glorious safari parks. We spent a week on the magical remote Swahili island of Lamu, with its narrow winding streets free of cars, where veiled Muslim women wander seated on donkeys and fisherman sail white-masted dhows across the azure waters. We stayed in thatched huts on the snow-white beaches in Malindi, and toured the port city of Mombasa, with its mix of Arabic and African peoples. As we stayed by the Indian Ocean and felt the ancient exotic Arab-influenced society along the coast, and the mysterious Swahili culture where women still veil their faces and live lives segregated from men, we slowed down and let the enormous cultural differences penetrate our beings. A weeklong trip to the idyllic island of Mauritius, far out in the Indian Ocean, an unexpected R&R allowed us following the bombing, comforted us like a soothing balm after a year of trauma and grief.

On numerous occasions, we went to the Masai Mara, driving through the magnificent indentation in the earth's crust called the rift valley, or up to the tea-rich Central Highlands, and on to towering Mount Kenya. The innumerable lodges in Kenya are rich in their diversity. We could choose among world-class tented safari camps, stilted lodges in the trees, elegant old country clubs, and exotic bush resorts just a breath away from wild animals. As residents of Kenya, we could drive any weekend to a different world-class resort but pay the much lower in-country rates.

Caroline and Christopher would pick up some Swahili words and mixed with fascinating guests from all parts of the world. Our children became quite accustomed to sleeping in the bush, spotting lions and cheetahs in the wild, and trekking in the wee hours of dawn to spot rare birds as the sun rose over the Serengeti. We slept in luxury tents, some with sunken bathtubs and four-poster beds, surrounded by the grunting sounds of hippopotami hovering just below the river's surface outside our tent, or with lions roaming our camp as we slept in beds warmed by hot water bottles. Sometimes we tried rustic camps with few amenities, with only a flap of canvas separating us from the wild game. We rented houses near volcanic lakes filled with flamingos, walked through paleontological digs searching for bone chips millions of years old, and went on walking safaris mingling with zebras, wildebeests, and giraffes. We were thrilled to see lions stalking a kill and birds bigger than Caroline. We took horseback rides through fields of wild game and viewed Mt. Kilimanjaro from our bedroom window.

As Hemingway and Dinesen have written, Africa has a way of getting under your skin; it fills your spirit, and experiencing it changes you. Each trip so full of adventure left us with countless memories and tales to tell. Our final trip was the most memorable, perhaps because we knew we would soon be leaving Kenya. After the exhausting year following the bombing, we and three other families decided to go on one last safari through Kenya's remote northern plains that run up to the Ethiopian border. Our route was incredibly rugged, the road nonexistent in places. Our caravan of Land Rovers crossed dry riverbeds and climbed over rocks, passing by nomadic tribes of Masai and Somali peoples, who silently stared at us as we passed.

After journeying many hours in the seemingly uninhabitable hill country, we arrived at a site in the bush called "Il Ngwesi." Perched high on a cliff, this was an "eco-lodge" run by a Masai tribe called the Ndorobo. Created partially by a grant from the U.S. Agency for International Development, it is managed by the tribe. Twelve Masai men dressed in their traditional bright red robes and holding long spears, stood waiting for us at the foot of the mountain on which their lodge perched. After such a journey, it was a sight to behold. They carried our bags up the winding path to Il Ngwesi lodge, which consisted of several secluded private huts dug into the hillside, constructed of natural wood without walls or windows. Each individual hut, designed as a natural extension of the mountain, formed its own lovely niche. Completely separated from the other lodges, we slept overlooking thousands of acres of open forest and mountains, whose silence was pierced by the occasional call of a leopard. Reveling in the silence and beauty, we showered outdoors under a rock outcropping. We brought our own food; the lodge staff prepared each meal in elegant fashion and served us banquets by candlelight under the moon. One of our group, Bobby, a musician from the cast of "Red Hot and Blue," played his guitar by a large rock swimming pool that flowed naturally over the edge of a cliff. By sunlight we swam, and in the moonlight we sang for hours by the fireside. Our voices floated over vast stretches of land where only wild animals could hear us.

The Masai warriors enchanted all the children, letting them hold their spears and thrilling them with tales about the wild animals in the forest. For each of us, those five days far from the troubles of the world proved profound. Stunned by how removed our lives had become from this kind of natural existence, we discovered how living in the wild filled a longing we all had deep inside.

One morning we arose at 4 a.m. and mounted a string of camels. Five-year-old Caroline was a bit frightened getting up on the camel, especially when the camel stood up, throwing her first face down, then horizontal in the opposite direction with her back to the ground. She screamed as her camel rose to full height. Once we were all mounted, we rode several hours deep into the bush, all the while spotting numerous fresh animal footprints, including those of elephant and lion. A quiet riverbank with a stunning view of Mount Kenya awaited us. There, the Masai built a fire and cooked a full breakfast for us. My Southern husband, Jim, even provided them with good ol' grits from South Alabama, which they simmered over the fire under his supervision. The children romped along the river in the shadow of Mt. Kenya, and bantered with the Masai guide-cooks, asking them what it was like to be a real warrior. Our camels waited patiently, munching shrubs while we ate. On the return journey, we sighted large herds of elephants and passed nomadic tribes of Somalis crossing the northern desert.

All of us on this trip to Il Ngwesi felt the magic of Kenya in its pure state. It is truly a garden that God created full of beauty, power, and elegance. We hated to return to Nairobi and our houses with walls, doors, and locks closed off from this natural beauty, after a week of open-air living.

During our last month and a half in Nairobi I focused on organizing our move back to the United States. Sorting our belongings, giving away toys to missions, running a big yard sale, supervising the packers, and bidding good-bye to friends, kept me occupied, as we slowly prepared ourselves mentally and emotionally for the return to America. Although we had done this many times, the process is never easy; rather it is long and arduous, yet cathartic and cleansing in its own way.

During our years in Kenya, we had been through a life-changing event, one that brought our friends extremely close to us. To say farewell, we invited friends to meet us for "Sundowners" in the Nairobi National Game Park south of the city. Under a spreading acacia tree, we gathered where we could see the rolling savanna, the Ngong Hills rumpled along the skyline, and the brilliantly orange sun setting over them. Our cook, Rose, and ayah, Nancy, came dressed in ceremonial African garb and cheerfully served drinks to the guests, while a caterer passed around bitings. The throb of African music drifted over the gathered herd of Land Rovers and four-wheel-drive vehicles, while the sunset melted into the African sky. In the golden yellow late afternoon sunshine, our crowd of friends ate and drank and reminisced, while wild rhinos roamed across the savannah in the far distance. It was a wonderful way to say good-bye to friends and to Kenya, on a magical evening in the game park just on the edge of the burgeoning and increasingly violent city of Nairobi.

As a final gesture before departure, several embassy friends and I purchased a park bench for the Nairobi Game Park as a memorial to Louise Martin, our dear friend who had died in the bombing. Louise was, like me, an "unofficial diplomat." She had never been paid for the work she did, but she had done much for our community and for Kenya. Louise had freely shared her skills in veterinary medicine and rescued many injured baby animals in the Nairobi Game Park. She was a volunteer at the animal orphanage and nursed starving baby elephants back to life, as if she were their mother. Many of us who had been in the Embassy bombing gathered that day in the park to say farewell, not only to Louise but to all the colleagues we were leaving behind, and to Kenya itself. Sitting on Louise's bench overlooking the golden expanse of land before me, I played guitar and sang Louise's favorite song, "From a Distance, God is Watching Us." We had all been through a moment in history that we would never forget; and a part of Louise, and of us all, will always remain lingering on that hillside in the Nairobi Game Park.

At last, our house was empty, car sold, and dog Jingles lodged in a kennel on a farm in Karen to be sent to Washington, D.C., a month later. Julia, the turtle, went to the Nairobi Museum Zoo, where Christopher and Caroline were certain she would live happily ever after with many fellow turtles. We transported the fish, splish-splashing, back to the Nakumat Fish store from whence they had come. The children each had big farewell parties with their friends, and we sadly said good-bye to our staff. In late June 1999, we boarded a plane and flew away from Kenya.

Until I sat on that plane with Jim, Christopher, and Caroline, I never realized the stress we had been living under. We were filled with an incredible sense of relief as our airplane left Africa behind. Although I loved so much about our life in Kenya, the crime and the bombing had been a constant pressure. I looked at Christopher and Caroline, still so small, just five and eight years old, and realized that I was so glad to be taking them back to a safer world. Who knows what remnants of this time in Kenya and of the bombing will come back to them in later years. I hope only the good memories.

Yes, our adventures had been many and wonderful, but I was thankful that we were all going home in one piece and together! Africa had changed us, and despite all, I was and am so grateful for the opportunity to get to know the place that is Africa. It will no longer just be a remote land mass on a map, but will remain deep in our hearts and minds forever, a memory full of passion and trauma, fear and freedom, and enduring beauty.

5
Back in the USA

Moving back to the United States in late 1999 after almost a decade abroad, I felt like Dorothy hurled by a tornado into Oz. When we landed, it sure didn't look like Kansas. I had expected moving back to the United States would be simple after all the moves we'd made; but moving is never easy, and this time was no easier, maybe even harder than other moves. We are Americans, but our children had never lived in America. We had been living in places with limited cultural choices, only a few government television channels, few or no supermarkets, scarce and rather poor daily newspapers, few cell phones, and only rudimentary Internet. We had lived with telephones so impossibly bad that the only way to communicate was to visit friends in person and talk over a cup of tea! Time moved much more slowly, and we grew to accept and even enjoy this simplicity of life.

Returning to America after so long a sojourn abroad, I confronted the dramatic contrasts. Arriving at New York's JFK International Airport, I found everyone frantically chatting on cell phones in their ears as they ran almost panicked through the corridors. "Wow," I thought, "I really have been away!" There had been very few cell phones in Kenya, while in the United States they were omnipresent. The change became more apparent later, as we drove past rows and rows of unsightly fast food joints and mammoth megastores like Wal-Mart, Best Buy, Home Depot, Toys R Us, one after the other, all surrounded by huge parking lots full of extremely oversized SUVs. Some people would call this progress. I found it depressing after village life in Kenya and India; because somehow in the rush to get ahead, America had left graciousness and taste behind.

As we drove on the highways, packed with drivers in their fancy utility vehicles, all in a seemingly perpetual rush, I asked Jim incredulously, "Where is everyone rushing at two o'clock on a Sunday afternoon?"

But it really hit me when we took the children into their first McDonald's, and a woman behind us was chastising her children via her cell phone. "Now stop fighting! I told you to do your homework! I am getting your dinner and I will be home soon. You are going to be in big trouble!" she screamed.

"Is this what the American lifestyle has turned into?" I anxiously asked Jim.

"Maybe, we won't be staying in America too long," Jim laughed.

Readjusting to life in the United States proved more difficult than adjusting to life in Kenya, India, or China had been. People moved in such a rush. Everyone sported not only cell phones but also palm pilots. They were inundated by information: hundreds of television stations, too many cultural events, and more newspapers, journals, and magazines in a week than one could read in a year. The choices were overwhelming: how to pick which cereal to buy when there are forty brands to choose from, or how to decide *which* cultural events to go to, when it was impossible to even read all the information about them in order to decide. Not to mention e-life; one was expected to read one's e-mails and answer within minutes. The greatest change was the omnipresence of ".com." It was discombobulating just trying to catch up with the pace of everyday life in America. In their rush to get ahead, people seemed to have become remarkably more aggressive, harried, consumerist, and competitive and much less joyful.

We were greatly relieved, nonetheless, to leave the bombing of the American Embassy in Nairobi and the added fears of carjacking and robberies behind. Although the bombing remained omnipresent in the lives of everyone in Kenya during the year we stayed in its aftermath, we came back to an America that had already forgotten about it and knew little about Kenya to begin with.

It was hard to dive right into American life. A neighbor would introduce herself and say something like, "You better hurry up and sign your children up for soccer!" Or "Most summer camps are full, whatever will your children do this summer?"

My response came out not quite right. I felt out of sync and wanted to say, "I'm Joanne, and I was just in a bombing." I decided to slowly acclimate to the American fast lane. My children were not going to be over programmed; I was determined to let them enjoy playing outside after school as they had done in Kenya. Little did I know that few other children would be around with whom they could play, having been programmed by their parents with full-time activities.

I told my father soon after arriving, "Everyone here seems completely oblivious to the wider world outside. Rushing to get ahead, they have no idea that there are people who actually hate America."

"Whom do you mean?" he asked.

"Well, take many in the Muslim world, for example, especially the Sudanese we bombed last year. There are many people who dislike our commercialism, our trashy movies, our military might, and our self-righteous attitude, and they are determined that our culture not 'pollute' theirs," I remorsefully said to my father. "I feel worried watching everyone blithely going off to Best Buy or Home Depot and spending money recklessly. They seem to have no sense that the world outside is very different, even hostile towards us, nor do they seem to care."

"Do you really think it is that bad? Things here are better than ever! What should we be doing differently?" my father countered.

Following the bombing in Kenya, I was leery of being recognized as an American. Afraid of being targeted again, I had removed our diplomatic license plates from our four-wheel-drive car and driven around for a whole year in Nairobi with no plates at all. No one ever noticed or stopped us—so much for Kenyan law and order! When someone came up to me on the street and asked, "Are you American?" I replied in German, *"Nein, bitte,"* and quickly moved on.

But now we had returned to the U.S.A., and despite our reverse culture shock, our only option was to try to fit back into American life. One saving grace was that we moved into a cozy traditional neighborhood in Bethesda, Maryland, called Wood Acres, which still maintained a Norman Rockwell 1950s atmosphere. Children played in the street and ran from house to house after school. We could walk to the local elementary school down the street and across the beautiful, grassy Wood Acres Park, where community life was centered. People gathered in the park in the evening, chatted, borrowed eggs, and watched each other's children. At Halloween and Christmas the neighborhood was festooned with decorations. Little had changed in fifty years, except that every house had an addition with a huge family room/kitchen and master bedroom and a new SUV in the driveway. Wood Acres was our buffer from the new high-tech, fast, competitive America, which we had to enter bit by bit. The professional transition was challenging. Jim experienced the change more dramatically than I. He went from being a U.S. diplomat, treated with deference and respect overseas and viewed as the embodiment of the United States of America, to becoming just one of tens of thousands of Washington bureaucrats working for the government. True to his predilection for crises, Jim became a member of the East Timor Task Force at State Department. Then, he became senior officer on the South East Asia Desk, responsible for dealing with narcotics proliferation, human trafficking, Agent Orange, and POWs. After a year, he was promoted to deputy director of the East Asia and the Pacific (EAP) Regional Office, where he organized regional meetings for Secretary of State Colin Powell with foreign ministers of Asian nations. Biking to work daily from Bethesda to Washington along the Capital Crescent trail, Jim constantly tried to maintain a balance between his work and his family. Work often won out, as it often does in the State Department, and we, his family, had to cope with his absence.

A Year and a Half In

I wish I could say that I settled in easily, but I did not. After having been back in the United States a year, on the surface all was well. Christopher and Caroline were doing well. They attended Wood Acres Elementary School, swapped pokemon cards, rode bicycles, and adapted to American life. I was living close to my extended family. Though daily life was calm, safe, and perhaps a bit boring, life in the United States felt like one long effort to keep up. Deep in my gut, I knew there were alternative ways to live, and the thought lingered and made my spirit restless.

Having lived through the events in Kenya, life had become more profound and precious. I was clear that my highest priority was to my children and to making their lives comfortable and stable, and that was a responsibility I took seriously. At first, I found myself more comfortable with foreigners than with my fellow countrymen. I was keenly aware of foreigners trying to adjust to and integrate into our community. They had a look in their eyes with which I could empathize. Was it fear, loneliness, homesickness, disorientation, or longing? I remember in particular one little Chinese girl who waited in line for school to start, all alone. The other children did not speak with her, ignoring her as they played. She hid her face in her Chinese book and pretended it didn't matter that she had no friends; but it broke my heart, and I knew very well that it hurt hers. One day I saw a child sobbing and holding onto her mother, not wanting to go into school. She and her family had just moved to the United States from Zambia. School was terrifying, so many changes at once, and she was all alone. I talked with her and tried to console her. She was so excited when I told her that I, too, had lived in Africa.

I often wondered if what we do to our children and to ourselves by living this global existence is good in the end. Is it character building, or does it scar us? Will understanding the world help us cope with the unknown global future, or is that lost sense of security irreparable? Did I not hope that the little girl from China and the little girl from Zambia were somehow integrated into our school and integrated in mind and spirit with where they were living? I suppose I did. And yet, what would happen when they had to leave and go back to their original culture? I wasn't sure how much change can be tolerated before it splinters the spirit. We need to be adaptable. Jim and I wanted our children to be tolerant of differences and ready for the global future. Yet, we also somehow needed to pass on a sense of rootedness as a foundation for conviction, confidence, and effectiveness. Were we able to do this with our globally mobile lifestyle? I often wished that there would be some easy remedy to help people in transition cope and move on. I know only too well, however, that each time it is hard work and takes every ounce of concentration one can muster.

That realization is why I chose to continue to work in the relocation and cross-cultural adjustment business. After returning to Washington from Kenya, I joined a consulting firm in Reston, Virginia, named Full Circle International and began to help foreigners adapt to life in the United States. This was somewhat ironic, because I was simultaneously having my own difficulties readapting.

Breaking through Glass

On August 7, 2001, we had been back in the United States for almost two years. As on any other day, I prepared Caroline and Christopher for camp, walked them to their bus, and then took our dog to her favorite field in lovely Wood Acres Park, where I met my dog-walking friends. Later that day, Dick Buckley, my friend from Kenya, called and asked, "How are you doing on this third anniversary?" It was a jarring question. I had actually forgotten the bombing three years earlier, and the heaviness had finally slipped from my back. After almost two years, I was finally beginning to enjoy comfortable suburban life in Bethesda.

Just one month later, however, on a perfect early fall morning with clear blue cloudless skies, I had, as usual, taken Jingles for her walk in the field behind our neighborhood school. Suddenly, a jogger raced up to me and hysterically shouted, "Go home quickly. New York City has just been attacked!"

My heart sank to my stomach, as the worst-case scenarios raced through my mind. I ran frantically home and anxiously turned on the television. As I watched NBC, I saw a most unfathomable thing happen—a plane had crashed intentionally into New York's World Trade Center. Then, as I was watching live, a second plane unbelievably crashed into the second tower. Television news commentators were shaken with shock and disbelief at what they were witnessing. It was like some kind of horror movie. The phone rang. It was my dear friend Sue Bartley, who had lost her husband and son in the bombing in Nairobi, breathlessly asking, "Joanne, are you alright? Turn on the television, Osama is at it again!"

"My God, I can't believe it, Sue, and you were living in the World Trade Center until just last week," I whispered "This is beyond belief! Sue, we may have a role to play here, helping people through this."

Stunned, we both hung up the phone. Sue had been in New York on and off for most of the previous year, attending the *U.S. vs. Osama bin Laden"* trial of the suspects in the bombing of the U.S. Embassies in Kenya and Tanzania, in the First District of New York. The U.S. government had invited victims and family members of victims to witness the trial, oddly enough putting them up at the Marriott Hotel at the base of the World Trade Center. I had stayed there for only one week, while Sue had stayed for much of the year, not missing a moment of the trial of those who had murdered her family.

During the day, we came face to face with the men who had plotted and bombed our Embassy in Nairobi. The passive expressionless faces of these short, slender men, staring past us as we silently watched the trial, left us empty and unsettled. We had each come to New York to tell our part of the story and listen to the trial proceedings. We saw and heard wiretapped recordings that linked Osama bin Laden directly with the 1993 attempt to blow up the World Trade Center. Then, we returned each night to sleep in that very building! This odd choice of hotel had made me anxious enough to avoid having a drink on the top floor. I had asked Sue if we could go out in the evening to Soho, rather than up to Windows on the World.

By September 11th, the trial had just ended, most of the witnesses and victims of the Nairobi bombing had left New York a week earlier, and the verdict of life imprisonment had been delivered. The sentencing was due to happen any day. Then, on September 11, I watched as the World Trade Center itself was blown up and collapsed into dust, killing more than 3000 people. Moments later, a third plane crashed into the Pentagon, and newscasts reported that another plane was headed for Washington, D.C., to an undetermined destination, maybe the White House, the Capitol, or the State Department.

Where was Jim? I called the State Department, but couldn't reach him. According to news reports, the State Department was being evacuated. Television news announcers said that there might be a car bomb in front of the building. I didn't know what to do. Memories of our Kenyan attack came rushing back to me— the screams, the smell of cement, the confusion—I could feel the adrenalin rushing through my body. At this very moment, a twelve-foot high window in our family room exploded into a million pieces. Thinking Washington itself had been attacked, fear ran through my veins. Should I run and get my children out of school? In a panic, I ran outside, not knowing what to do next.

The neighbor's gardener was sheepishly standing there trying to tell me something, as tears streamed down my face. "Madam, I think a rock shot off from my lawn mower and cracked your window," he shyly said.

"What did you say?" I screamed.

"It was a rock," he peeped.

"You mean Washington is not being hit?!" I yelled. Not having seen the news, he had no idea what I was talking about. Relieved, I threw my arms around him. He thought I was nuts.

Several neighbors and my sister, Christine, came to be with me and watch the horrendous news unfold on the television screen. Finally, Jim called to assure me that he was all right and was making his way home on the Metro, packed with nervous people. Without being told what was going on, Caroline and Christopher were sent home from school on the school bus. Wanting to shelter them from fear, Jim and I met them at the bus stop and explained the events unfolding as we walked home. The days that followed were reminiscent of the aftermath of the Kennedy assassination, when everyone in the nation was in shock, glued to the television with tears in their eyes.

I know my experience is just one of millions on September 11th. What gnawed at me, however, was that in the year after we had returned from Kenya, I had had a feeling about the world and the United States. I knew terror, and I knew America was a target, but I hadn't talked to people about my fears. I knew something else could easily happen. Should I have been out speaking more about my experience in Kenya? Could I have warned people about what might happen? Who could have predicted this level of insanity?

After September 11, everyone in America felt a need to respond somehow. How could I help those suffering because of the attacks in New York and Washington? The most important lesson I had learned from Kenya was that it is vital to communicate. We all needed to talk endlessly about what happened in New York and Washington on September 11th. We needed to discuss the events from every angle. Only after all the feelings have been shared can healing begin.

It is so important to communicate with those who are suffering. It is very hard to visit or call a friend who just lost her husband or his wife, but it is crucial to do so. I learned through experience that it is much better to say anything at all, to show you care and to offer your support, than to stay away in fear of doing or saying the wrong thing. Those who came to me, called me, and supported me after the Nairobi bombing, are indelibly etched in my mind. So, too, are the ones, who, for whatever reason, said nothing to me, didn't call, and didn't come. It hurt then, and it is hard to forget that they were not there.

A Changed Nation

The first few weeks following September 11 were hard for America and for me. Yet, I began to see visible, positive changes in the country. A strong sense of community grew where none had been before. People seemed more open and a bit humbler in their vulnerability, families and neighbors more united. Even the frantic consumerism seemed to abate a little. Perhaps in some ironic way, some good came out of September 11.

One evening in the week following the attacks, I received several e-mail messages urging people to light a candle, for the victims of September 11th, at seven p.m. on the night of September 18th. I told my daughter, "I don't want to light a candle alone. Let's invite the neighbors to join us."

"Okay, Mommy, I'll help," she responded and designed a small flyer that we slipped under the front doors of each house on our block. At seven p.m., we went out in the street with our two candles.

"Mommy," Caroline cried, "Look at all the people coming outside!" There were almost a hundred people, ranging in age from ten-month-old William to eighty-five-year-old Joe Hintersehr, a reclusive man hardly known by the neighbors, who came out using his walker. We all joined hands and sang "God Bless America," then lit one candle and silently passed the flame around the circle from person to person. I led a short prayer and others joined in with their own prayers. It was all the more poignant because Hamilton Peterson, who lived across the street from us, had lost his father and stepmother on Flight 93, which crashed in a field in Pennsylvania, a crash that perhaps saved the lives of many people in Washington. Every person in that circle was with Hamilton in sympathy that night.

Finally, a tiny boy named Patrick asked, "Can we sing 'Jose, can you see'?" Everyone laughed, and we did our best to reach the high notes of our national anthem. "The bombs bursting in air, gave proof through the night that our flag was still there." A warm and unified feeling spread among the neighbors and within minutes of walking home, almost every house on our block had hung out an American flag. There was a tremendous surge of patriotism that night on Harwick Road in Wood Acres, Bethesda, Maryland, U.S.A., probably not too different from neighborhoods across America in those days after 9/11.

Later that week, eight-year-old Caroline wrote a letter to Rose, our housekeeper back in Kenya. "You know those people who were trying to kill us in Kenya, Rose?" she wrote. "Well, now they are here!" Sadly, I worried that Caroline and Christopher would spend their whole lives worrying about terrorism and Osama Bin Laden. How awful to live with such fear.

The American people bore a heavy weight, especially in Washington, where the Pentagon had been attacked, and who knows what other building had been missed by the plane that crashed in Pennsylvania. An enveloping sense of ever-present danger lingered inside the hearts and minds of people in Washington. For days, we heard the roar of F-16 fighter jets overhead at all times of the night and day. Newspapers continued to warn of possible nuclear, biological, or chemical attacks. Letters filled with Anthrax spores were sent to Capitol Hill, the National Post Office, and the State Department. Jim continued to go to work at the department with the thought that maybe that day Washington would be attacked. He painstakingly went over our life insurance policy with me in detail before he left for work one day, not knowing what might happen. The next month, the United States attacked Afghanistan to try to rout out the Al Qaeda terrorists. The world seemed full of violence.

It felt as though our country were at war. Our president called it "a war on terrorism." In our nation's capital, we had the feeling that, once again, as in the cold war, we were living at Ground Zero. Heightened security protected the city and the president, and we were constantly reminded of how precarious this game of war is. Although the sun was shining, there were clouds of doubt in each person's mind.

But how do people full of fear learn the most pressing lesson of terrorism? In order not to give in to the terrorists, it is important not to be afraid, but to communicate, not only with each other, but internationally with people of other nations and to continue to travel abroad. It is vitally important for Americans of all ages, colors, and races to be visible around the world. I wanted to shout that, despite the difficulties, this was not a time to avoid travel, but perhaps a most important time to be truly international. It is so important for Americans to personally meet Middle Easterners, Asians, Europeans, and Africans. It is important to communicate in informal, non-arrogant ways that we are a unique and wonderful people and not the evil empire the terrorists paint us to be. We must truly try to understand people of other cultures. Each of us, one on one, whether at home or abroad, should try to make friends with people of other nations. Can you imagine if millions of Americans decided to travel or live abroad instead of staying isolated in America?

One lesson we must take from the attacks of September 11 is that we know shockingly little about people of other cultures, and they too little of us. We must fight the impulse to protect ourselves by running the other way to isolate ourselves. We have been remiss in communicating the essence of America to the world. We cannot leave it to the diplomats, the media, or the military. Every one of us is an "unofficial diplomat" who must turn outward, not inward. Every one of us must try to communicate better inside and outside our borders, the United States and everywhere. And in so doing, the world may start to heal.

6

To Move or Not to Move, That Is the Question

In late 2003, just two years after September 11, our family faced the decision whether to continue in the Foreign Service and go abroad again, leaving the comfort of our Wood Acres community. There was so much to weigh in deciding. Our children were by then fully adjusted to life in America. They liked the United States, and they didn't want to move again and leave their neighborhood and friends for uncertainty. Our home was wonderfully comfortable after we remodeled it, creating a big bright kitchen and family room addition on the back, and each room exactly as we wanted. Schooling had become more and more important as the children got older. Caroline would be going into sixth grade and Christopher into ninth. Should we leave the United States now that Caroline was in middle school? Should we wait until they were both in high school? Should we leave at all? We debated the options ad infinitum.

One fall evening, Jim and I went to a dinner for our friends from India, the Keavenys, where the guests were all in the Foreign Service or related international agencies. The colorful crowd of Americans talked about their children who were able to speak Arabic, Spanish, French, and Chinese. Watching the assembled children, I realized they would be so much better positioned to cope with and contribute to the world in the future that we are just beginning to imagine than children who lived only in the States, sheltered, speaking no foreign languages, and rarely meeting people from different cultures.

What did we want for Christopher and Caroline? In the short term, with terrorism at its height, it seemed crazy to go out to work in an American Embassy. Why place our family and children in harm's way yet again? Why act as fodder for more terrorist actions? But, would we actually be less safe abroad? Perhaps now that terrorism had come to our shores, there were no safe places to live. We needed to be able to understand the world, and it is hard to do that sitting in Bethesda, Maryland, or anywhere in America for too long. As the wife of an American diplomat, I again had the opportunity to represent my country in another nation. Would I have the courage to go this time, and when asked if I am an American, would I be able to proudly reply, "Yes, I am"?

The five years from 1999 to 2004 had not been easy times. Americans had the world come crashing in on them on September 11. Not long ago, it was easy to visit Starbucks and chat optimistically about house-buying, politics, or the stock market. After 2001, Iraq, Pakistan, North Korea, and Afghanistan were in Americans' everyday vocabulary. Today, Americans worry about the instability of Pakistan, the person of Osama bin Laden, the crimes of Saddam Hussein and Kim Jong Il. President George W. Bush, who upon taking office appeared to know little about the world, was faced with the most pressing international crises of our time, which have forced most Americans into a heightened concern about international relations. Although President Bush may have preferred to act unilaterally, in the end he had no choice but to work multinationally in fighting terrorism. The world is rapidly shrinking, and Americans are finally being drawn into the mix, for better or worse. We can no longer close our eyes or our borders.

Adding to the stress of the fight against terrorism, or perhaps to divert attention from its inability to capture Osama bin Laden, our government launched a full-fledged, unprovoked war with Iraq. The administration made a modest attempt to include other nations in its plans. They organized something called "the coalition of the willing," which included such countries as Vanuatu, Kiribati, and Palau. Several U.N. resolutions demanded Iraq rid itself of its weapons of mass destruction, with warnings of dire consequences to follow if they did not. The dire consequences followed: war.

Destroying much of the good will we had received from nations all over the world after 9/11, and in spite of objections from these same nations and the reluctance of the U.N. Security Council, our government bombed Iraq and destroyed the government of Saddam Hussein, shocking the world. Since then, nothing has remained the same.

While the UN debated the Iraq crisis, at home Jim and I argued and disagreed vehemently about the U.S. position on Iraq. I was totally against our unilateral invasion and vehemently opposed to military bullying.

At home, I would sarcastically jibe at Jim, "You are the diplomat. Why can't you think of other strategies for dealing with Iraq than military ones? Is diplomacy dead?"

Jim responded with the WMD argument. If Saddam Hussein had WMD, as the intelligence indicated, then no one was safe.

Jim thought I was naïve and uninformed. I granted him that Saddam Hussein was evil. But there are many evils in the world, and somehow using force, killing, and destruction to attack evil in another nation would never be acceptable to me and would, in the long run, prove counterproductive. I have seen destruction and know it only breeds resentment and hurt, takes years to get over, if ever, and always begets more violence. During this time, I joined Peace marches in Washington, while Jim rushed off to work at six a.m. to plan for war contingencies and postwar reconstruction. Our family was reflecting the world turmoil.

Caroline and Christopher didn't want to hear too much about our views on Iraq. They begged Jim and me to stop arguing with each other about it. They didn't like to look at the news or read the newspapers, since they were full of Iraq and Osama bin Laden. News stories showed one bomb incident after another, each reminiscent of what we experienced in Nairobi, and each so senseless. Despite their growing up with Osama bin Laden, my kids are like kids everywhere in the world. They just want to have fun and live their lives. I was sad that so much tension surrounded them. They couldn't help but take it in. I don't remember the tensions ever being as high at any time in my life as at this time.

Unable to contain my feelings, I wrote an op-ed piece against the bombing of Iraq, which appeared as a full-page article in the

Washington Post one April morning several days after the U.S. attacks on Iraq began.

This is what it said:

> I am horrified as I read in the newspapers about the Iraqi families who have been bombed in their homes by the United States and who are reeling from the shock. I am immediately thrust back to the moment in 1998 in Nairobi, Kenya, when I was in the basement of the U.S. Embassy with my two small children and we were bombed by al Qaeda cohorts of bin Laden. . . .
>
> How could such an act of inhumanity happen, I wondered in my sorrow and confusion. The Iraqi people caught in their own homes, while minding their own business, must be asking the same question.
>
> My conclusion after being attacked in Nairobi was that we Americans had every obligation to bridge the gap of misunderstanding and to try to communicate and learn about the anger directed at us. Being the wife of a diplomat, I felt that diplomacy was needed more than ever, to open up dialogue and find resolution to our conflicts with Muslim nations. I felt that not only formal diplomacy but also informal diplomacy, the kind that I and other Americans living abroad practice every day, was of utmost importance if we were ever to begin to find a way toward solutions to our misunderstandings. . . .
>
> Rather than expanding our diplomatic efforts, we have stopped them, in favor of bombing. We resorted to bombs and military attacks in an all-out effort to stop the hatred against our people.
>
> But I am certain that bombs only exacerbate anger and pain and confusion and terror, and it grieves me to see that we are doing to other innocent people exactly what was done to us in 1998. You are wrong, Mr. President, if you think this will heal the anger against us. You are wrong, Mr. Rumsfeld, if you think you can bomb away terror. You are wrong, Mr. Cheney, if you think this will all be over soon.

As a member of one family that survived a bomb, I can tell you from the bottom of my heart: Bombing will never be the solution. Do you think the Iraqi families you are bombing today are going to get up and thank you and want to know more about our great country? You are wrong.

The reaction I received was overwhelming—about sixty people who didn't even know me called to say they were in total agreement with my article. People I had never met—former soldiers and diplomats, priests, and private citizens—called to say they had been afraid to speak out against the war in Iraq. In America! Jim was taken off guard. Although I did mention it to him, he never thought that I, the wife of a Foreign Service officer, would so blatantly, on a full-page column in the *Washington Post,* publicly denounce our government's plan to bomb another nation without provocation. Even our congressman's wife called to say how courageous she thought I was to go public with my opposition to the war.

Although he took a few jibes from his colleagues at the State Department, Jim never got angry with me but took it in stride. The morning my column appeared in the *Washington Post*, Jim arrived at Under Secretary Marc Grossman's office for the post–Iraq war reconstruction meeting that he attended each morning as the East Asia Bureau representative. Several colleagues around the room pointedly noted, "We saw your wife's editorial in the *Post*, Jim."

One of the most disastrous results of the bombing of Iraq is that many nations no longer trust the United States. This type of foreign policy has destroyed our nation's reputation throughout the world. Although Jim is still in the Foreign Service, there are few safe places and fewer friendly places to serve as diplomats anymore. When I traveled around Europe in the 1970s, I felt wonderful being an American. Everyone wanted to talk with me; and despite the war in Vietnam, most said we had a great country. It is different today. Even though the entire world was empathetic with America after September 11, thanks to George Bush's policy on Iraq many people genuinely hate America, and many are lining up to hurt us. This has caused all Americans, not only those abroad, but those at home as well, to feel significantly less safe in this world. Our so-called war on terrorism has bred hundreds of terrorist acts and countless thousands of new terrorists.

The war and turmoil have not ended as quickly as President Bush promised. Americans and people of other nations that aid our efforts in Iraq are continually attacked. Americans are dying every week in Iraq. Our newspapers are filled with daily bombings, showing body parts flying. My heart is heavy watching the violence that has spread like wildfire around the world—one violent act begetting another.

Numerous American embassies have been the targets of planned attacks that luckily have thus far been thwarted. American journalists have been targeted. Some, like Daniel Pearl of the *Wall Street Journal*, have been killed. Diplomats and their families have been murdered in Pakistan and Jordan. Foreigners have been kidnapped. Small terrorist acts have occurred all over the world in American resorts, in bars, at U.S. consulates, at military bases, and at airports. Terror floods the newspapers.

In 2003 and 2004, there was an unreal quality to living in Washington, D.C. I would sit at breakfast with my children, while in the background the radio warned us that we might have a terrorist attack at any time, "Today is a code orange alert," but "please continue to go about your life as normal," the announcer would ironically say. Remarkably, despite an all-out assault by the American military in Afghanistan, Osama bin Laden has not yet been caught. He remains somewhere out there, laughing at us all. I had experienced his brand of evil in Nairobi in 1998. By 2003 everyone in America feared it, without knowing fully what to fear. For a while, tourists were wary of visiting our national monuments on the Smithsonian mall. Once the pride of our nation, they had become potential targets for terrorists.

At one time, on the recommendation of the U.S. Department of Homeland Security, Americans flooded the hardware stores, trying to buy duct tape and plastic to cover their basement windows. Hysterically, we all began preparing for shelter from the terror, much like the bomb shelter hysteria of the 1950s. I, too, dutifully bought our own supply of duct tape and plastic. Jim laughed at the absurdity of the advice and used the plastic for one of his construction projects. Working at the State Department each day discussing the strategies for dealing with terrorism, Jim could not see how going down into the basement in a sealed-in room would solve anything. He was probably right. Yet, thoughts flooded my mind of how I would handle it if I were in the house with my children and their friends, when an attack occurred. Could I possibly feed them all for three or four days, did I have enough water, would we be able to communicate outside of the house, with their parents, with the world?

One day Caroline and I matter-of-factly prepared our bomb shelter in the basement, gathering enough food, water, and clothing for three days, checking flashlights and batteries for cordless radios. Everyone felt the urgency to become informed about how to deal with an attack. Many bought gas masks, cipro (antibiotics) to counter biological warfare, and walkie-talkies for communication. And yet, it is chaos that will probably cripple us. How crazy the world had become in just a few short years.

With the world in this state, Jim and I were faced with the decision of whether we should continue our life in the Foreign Service. Jim toyed with retiring from government and trying to work in the private sector. He talked with people in Washington about his options for consulting with a think tank. Though unsure, I held firmly to the belief that our family would benefit from living overseas again. I watched as my children grew up each day— Christopher taller than I, and Caroline a young lady. They had become so very American in their style. We were living the full American suburban existence; yet, I had my doubts about it. We had before us an opportunity to serve our country abroad again. We all had an option to learn more and open our minds to other cultures.

By October 2003, despite his pacifist wife, Jim was promoted in the Foreign Service. We decided that we should make a bid on overseas jobs and see what might come of it. In the Foreign Service, diplomats select from a list of Foreign Service jobs available worldwide at their rank and make a bid list of the countries and positions in which they want to serve. Then one waits and hopes that one of those jobs will be where you are eventually assigned. Hunting for places somewhat safe, Jim and I listed jobs in Auckland, Vienna, Taiwan, Perth, Johannesburg, and Beijing. We considered how we would live in each of these places—what schools the children would go to, what our home would be like, the safety factor, the friendliness of the people toward Americans. The bid process is a bit like riding a roller coaster; you are never sure where you are until it is over.

I waited with trepidation, not knowing how we would be able to make the transition to a new place. Those of us who accompany our diplomat spouses are not always privy to the intelligence information that might forewarn us of danger. We are not given much support for being on the front line. Yet, although we know there are risks, we keep going. The State Department is cautious about sending families to areas of high security risk. Many posts are now "unaccompanied" posts, which means that the families stay home while the officer leaves. The State Department is having trouble filling many posts in the hot spots of the world, like Iraq, Afghanistan, Lebanon, and Somalia. More and more, single diplomats and people without children are filling such posts. They are even offering these hard-to-fill jobs to Foreign Service spouses as if they were wonderful job opportunities.

All are required to receive pre-departure security training. Jim and I dutifully sat through the "Security Overseas Seminar" (SOS) and spent eight hours learning about the most horrendous scenarios that could possibly happen: carjacking, biological warfare, nuclear war, bombings, and kidnappings. It was such a lovely way to spend a day. Embassies all over the world are being fortified with new security walls, alarms, and procedures. Diplomats are being moved into compounds that provide more safety in numbers, higher walls, more guards, and bombproof windows. All of this is being done in an effort to protect us, but it also cuts us off from the people in the countries in which we serve, making it a bit hard to be good diplomats. Yet, despite all this, the Huskeys were considering going overseas again. Some would say we were crazy.

Diplomats and accompanying spouses, as well as American businesspeople, journalists, tourists, and students—all are valuable resources, a knowledge bank of the people of the world. By living and working in the various nations of the world, Americans grow in understanding and empathy, learn that people do things differently in different cultures, and know that things don't work the same way in Kabul as they do in Washington. If we are going to move forward in this global society, we desperately need this firsthand knowledge.

Most Americans who supported the bombing of Serbia or Iraq have most likely never met a Serb or an Iraqi. They certainly don't know how they live, how they think, how they work, and how they solve conflicts. But Americans living abroad do. They know the people. They are friends with them. They often speak their language, drink their drinks, play their sports, and dance their dances. At the same time they are the eyes and ears of America, informing the people and policy makers back home of the reality in the host country. Without this reality check, all we have left are people behind high walls looking at computers and radar screens with maps of Baghdad, Tora Bora, or wherever the latest conflict arises.

Worse yet, people around the world primarily receive their images of America from movies, television, music, and the Internet. For many people being an American means being a soldier, or a character in *Bay Watch* or the latest Hollywood movie. When we lived in India in 1993, it came as a big surprise to many people I met that I was nothing like Caroline in the television program *The Bold and the Beautiful*. While I had never even seen the show, this was their image of America. Every South Indian watched this program. For many, I was the first non-celluloid American they had ever met.

Equally amazed were the Kenyans whom I met and worked with after the bombing of our Embassy. Many themselves or their families were victims in the Embassy bombing. They were angry at what America did to them. They thought it was our fault that this trauma had happened to them. "If Americans had not been in our country, this tragedy would not have happened to us!" they cried. At first, when I told them my children and I were in the bombing and that we also were hurt, they couldn't believe Americans had suffered like them. When we shared our sadness and worked together to heal, they became less angry at America. We were all victims of that atrocity. We could have come away from the trauma in Kenya with more fear and more hatred, but getting to know one another helped build greater understanding. Only "ground troops" of regular, decent Americans can do that.

I have been an "unofficial diplomat" for twenty years, part of the unofficial ground troops, while Jim has been the official diplomat.

We both finally came to the realization that despite the huge risks, it was important to continue to live and serve abroad.

In February 2004, the State Department informed us that we were to go to Taiwan that August. An island of Chinese heritage and culture, Taiwan is modern and friendly, with few security risks (other than a possible war with China.) We sat down with Caroline and Christopher and discussed what our lives would be like. At first the kids were skeptical, like any kids. "What about our friends?" they asked. But we discussed it, and they came to feel Taiwan could be a great adventure for them, one that would open up the world, and one we couldn't afford to turn down. We all began to get excited and started to plan.

Barely a week after we heard of our assignment, however, Taiwan hit the front pages of every newspaper in the country. The Taiwanese president-elect was pressing for a referendum to be placed on the ballot that demanded China remove its missiles pointed at Taiwan. China was incensed and threatened war if Taiwan declared independence. Realizing the danger of this conflict, President Bush urged Taiwan not to hold the referendum. But Taiwan, realizing its chance to leverage independence, ignored the U.S. warning. The day before the presidential election, just three months before we were to move to Taiwan, the president and vice president of Taiwan were shot, though not killed, while campaigning for reelection. In late March of 2004, they won reelection by an extremely narrow margin, some said because of a sympathy vote. The referendum for Taiwan's independence, however, did not pass, so potential conflict was averted, at least for a while.

I queried Jim, "Of course, we won't go to Taiwan, will we, if there is a war with China?"

"Let's see what happens," Jim responded. "One thing we know for certain, Taiwan will not be boring, and if the United States can help prevent a war, we may be of use."

As we planned for our departure for Taiwan, terrorist acts continued to be aimed at Americans. In the United States, we were constantly on heightened alert, being warned that another major terrorist attack could happen at any time. I began to wonder if we would make it out of the country. I also wondered whether Taiwan would remain safe. The catch-22 of our situation did not negate my strong conviction that Americans need to break the walls of isolation and get out and understand the world.

Jim and I celebrated our eighteenth wedding anniversary that May. Over a lovely dinner at The Angler's Inn, an elegant restaurant in the Maryland suburbs, I mentioned to him that in the eighteen years we had been together, we had moved seven times. That was an average of one move every two and a half years! We have been busy! Our children have greatly complicated the equation, but over dinner, we decided we would go ahead and move to Taiwan.

In July, we said good-bye to our neighbors, friends, and family, once again shipped our cocker spaniel, Jingles, off to Taiwan ahead of us to spend her twenty-three days in quarantine, and packed up our things from the house on Harwick Road in Bethesda. We were, yet again, heading to the far side of the world.

Joanne with Kenyan children, Masai Mara, Kenya 1997.

Caroline on a camel, Malindi, Kenya 1997.

Caroline and Jingle Bells,
Kenya 1997.

On Safari at Karen, near Nairobi, Kenya 1997.

Joanne at home in Nairobi, 1998.

The Kenyan Huskeys, Kenya 1998.

The cast of *White Mischief*, Joanne seated right, Nairobi 1998.

At the Muthaiga Club, Jim and Joanne, Nairobi 1997.

Finding elephant tusks on safari in Samburu Game Park, Kenya 1999.

Archeological dig in the Rift Valley, Kenya 1999.

Christopher and a Masai warrior at Il Ngwesi, Kenya 1999.

Joanne greeting Marine guards at the Marine Corps Ball, Nairobi, 1998.

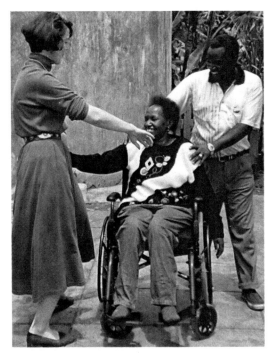

Joanne dancing in the Rift Valley with wheelchair-bound Teresa Karanja, a survivor of the Nairobi Embassy bombing, 1999.

Kenyan victims of the U.S. Embassy bombing with Joanne, Chair of American Women's Association, Nairobi 1999.

On the road to Il Ngwesi,
Christopher and Joanne,
Kenya 1999.

Dancing in the show
Red, Hot, and Blue,
Annalisa Allen (left)
and Joanne, Nairobi
1999.

Joanne receives an award from Ambassador Prudence Bushnell,
U.S. Embassy Nairobi, 1999.

Our Wood Acres home in Bethesda, Maryland, USA, Jim, Caroline, and Christopher, 2001.

Back in Washington, D.C., Joanne, Chris, and Caroline, 2002.

Jim and Joanne with Taiwan President Chen Shui Bian, Taipei, Taiwan, 2005.

Huskey family at Christopher's graduation from Taipei American School, 2008.

7

Isla Formosa (Beautiful Island)

There is something disconcerting about waking up in our home in suburban Washington, D.C., in the morning, and going to bed that evening in our new home on top of a mountain in Taiwan. We walked out of Chiang Kai-shek Airport in Taipei to find ourselves the only Caucasians in a sea of Chinese faces. With her red hair, Caroline stood out as we wove our way through the crowds in search of the driver sent to meet us. Taiwan is off the regular tourist route. With Hong Kong, China, Singapore, and Japan to chose from, few foreign visitors ever make it to Taipei. It was a shock to find ourselves such a minority in this pulsating, lively, but distinctly Chinese city. As our car wound through the streets bright with vertical neon signs in Mandarin, noodle shops on every corner, hundreds of people walking through the lively night markets, tea stalls filled with tea lovers, we gazed out of the car windows, each secretly wondering what our lives would be like there.

Taiwan's summer air was hot and the humidity oppressive, yet the city was teeming with thousands of people totally immersed and content on this Asian island. We found some relief as our car started to climb Yangmingshan (Yangming Mountain) that separates Taipei from the Pacific Ocean and the East China Sea. Our car climbed rapidly from the village of Tienmu, which lies in a valley on the northern outskirts of Taipei, along a narrow winding road as the lights of the city dropped far below. The road had hairpin turns and steep cliffs dropping precipitously on either side. We seemed to be in a traditional Chinese landscape painting, complete with steep mountains, teahouses hanging off cliffs, and pagodas and temples far in the distance surrounded by deep green foliage enveloped in mist. The views of Taipei city, while breathtaking as they twinkled far below, provided us all a sense of relief in their distance. As night fell, we arrived at our new home on top of the mountain, where the breezes from the Pacific gave us a reprieve from the heavy air of the city far below.

Taiwan seems to be one of the few countries in the world at the beginning of the twenty-first century where the people genuinely like Americans. And Taipei is one of the few cities in the world that are safe enough to walk through at night without fear of crime and where the people are extremely polite, honest, gentle, and friendly. So, we came to realize that we had landed in a pretty special place in the summer of 2004.

Unable to read signs or menus or to speak with people in the streets, I struggled through the first few strange weeks, trying desperately to remember the remnants of Chinese Mandarin I had retained from our years in Beijing. All four of us quickly began to study Mandarin trying to improve rapidly. It was interesting for Jim and me to see how our by then sixteen-year-old knowledge of Chinese, slowly came back to us.

Each of the four of us had major withdrawal symptoms on leaving the United States. We felt like square pegs being pushed into round holes. Not only weren't we sure we had made the right choice moving to this new location on the other side of the earth, but the usual culture shock and homesickness hit the children and me with a vengeance, sparing only Jim, who quickly went to work at the American Institute in Taiwan (AIT), the unofficial U.S. embassy in Taiwan. After seven major moves, it was surprising that moving was still so difficult. This time, moreover, we had two adolescents whose lives had been turned topsy-turvy. Jim and I questioned whether we had made the right choice moving to this new place. At night, we fretted and worried over what we had done to Christopher, who at fourteen, had to leave his friends and his thriving rock band to start all over in a strange, alien culture. Eleven-year-old Caroline suffered intense homesickness and loneliness, crying every night for weeks and begging us to return home to the U.S. To add to the adventure, Taiwan greeted us with two back-to-back typhoons and a small earthquake before school even got started. The first day of school was, in fact, cancelled because of one typhoon! In late

August, the weather was anything but welcoming—hot, humid, and constantly raining. Once again, the transition was just plain hard, and it took a while to shed our American skins and open up to the new adventure.

Jim had done his doctoral research in Taiwan thirty years before, and his memories of the island were strong and good. He wanted his family to love Taiwan. In the middle of one raging typhoon, he decided to show our children what the real Taiwan was like. He drove us up Yangmingshan through the howling wind to a small Japanese guest house that AIT owned. With the wind blowing at seventy miles an hour, and the rain pouring, he threw open all the windows of the house, put on Italian opera at full blast, and opened a bottle of wine. "This," he told us, "is Taiwan! Welcome to the *Isla Formosa!*" Sitting on the tatami mats of the Japanese house, wrapped in sleeping bags, cold and unhappy with the raging wind shaking the paper-thin walls, Christopher and Caroline looked at their parents as if they were absolutely crazy!

A few days later, the kids started at Taipei American School (TAS), one of the best international schools in the world. The school, vibrant with activity, colorful, and academically rigorous, quickly drew us in and helped to integrate us into life in Taipei. At first, both Chris and Caroline found it unsettling to be among the small handful of non-Asian students in their classes. Hearing Chinese and Taiwanese spoken in the cafeteria and hallways of TAS left them fearing they would never fit in. Gradually, though, they realized that many of these Asian kids were actually born in the United States or Canada, or were half Taiwanese, half Western. In addition to Taiwanese, there were Korean, Filipino, Malaysian, Singaporean, and Japanese students, and a small population of New Zealanders, Australians, Europeans, and Americans. The cultural mix of TAS, though not obvious at first glance because of the strong Asian presence, was actually rich with diversity.

Chris and Caroline began learning about Asia in the halls and classrooms of TAS, as well as in the streets of Taipei. The kids came home from school exclaiming, "You won't believe it, Mom, but it's really cool to be smart here!" The influence of Confucianism was still strong on this heavily traditional island. The students worked hard and behaved respectfully out of a desire to "please their ancestors." This produced a school full of aspiring students with respect for their elders.

The scope of education at TAS was quite remarkable. In his first year there, Chris had traveled to Hong Kong and Bangkok with our family, to Manila and Kuala Lumpur to compete as part of the TAS Tigers varsity swim team, to Cambodia with his ninth grade class, and to southern Thailand with the jazz band. In Cambodia, he learned about the Khmer Rouge atrocities and visited the magnificent temple city of Angkor Watt. After the tsunami hit South and Southeast Asia in December 2004, TAS responded by raising funds, and Chris went with his jazz band to work with the victims in Khao Lak, Thailand. In this fishing village completely destroyed by the tsunami, he delivered gift guitars and taught the newly orphaned children music in the evening, while helping rebuild a school and clean up the wreckage by day. Deeply moved by what he saw, he wrote and performed a song at the 100th Day Memorial of the tsunami. He returned to Taiwan ten days later, changed by the experience and ready to go back as soon as he could.

At TAS, Caroline made friends from Singapore, France, Taiwan, Malaysia, Canada, Australia, Philippines, and New Zealand. On her school breaks, she traveled with us to Hong Kong, Borneo, Thailand, Vietnam, China, Malaysia, Bali, Boracay Island in the Philippines, and the hinterland of Taiwan. She went with her drama group to Bangkok for an international theater conference, and to Kuala Lumpur with her touch rugby team. These were life-changing experiences that we could never have given them had we stayed in the United States.

TAS was one of the most dynamic schools I had ever seen, with active involvement by the parents. I ran for and won a place on the TAS Board of Directors. Deeply committed to international education, I became totally immersed in the life of this large and complex international school. TAS is a not just a full K–12 school with 2,200 children; it also serves as a community hub for all kinds of activity day and night. Students and parents are welcome to meet there and often congregate in the brightly lit lobby. It is a warm, welcoming place where students, teachers, staff, and parents are all equally respected and intermingle comfortably throughout the day.

After school and on weekends, the campus is filled with students performing music, dancing, practicing theater, and playing sports until late at night. TAS students raised in a multicultural and multilingual environment grow up with the knowledge that they will play a role as leaders in our global future. I saw my challenge, as a board member, was to sketch out what that future would be like and how TAS could prepare these children to succeed and contribute to a better world. By the time I left the board, we had built a four-story age-appropriate, multimedia learning center and changed the school into a one-on-one laptop environment. These improvements began to address the enormous changes the students would have to face in our ever-evolving global society.

Seeking to immerse myself in the traditional Chinese culture, I applied to serve as a docent at the National Palace Museum, one of the world's premier museums. There I studied about the thousands of years of Chinese imperial culture, art, and history—acquiring detailed knowledge of the jades, bronzes, porcelains, calligraphy, and painting collected by the Emperors of China going back 8,000 years. This knowledge, in turn, greatly enriched my life in Taipei. It gave me a context to appreciate the beauty of the art, the grace of the culture, and the symbolism of the customs. Everywhere I turned, remnants of ancient China were visible—in the auspicious symbols of the holidays, in the antique furniture of the homes, in the rituals of the temples, in the Confucian habits of the people. It was a special privilege to get to know up close the beautiful art pieces that the emperors themselves enjoyed and, in turn, to share this knowledge with English-speaking foreign visitors, both as a museum docent and through writing articles on Chinese culture for Taiwan English magazines.

Having been spared the antihistorical Cultural Revolution, Taiwan today retains a more authentic traditional Chinese culture than does mainland China. In Taiwan, ancient traditions are alive and exist side by side with a booming modern high-tech culture. Street-corner Buddhist and Taoist temples are filled with worshippers lighting incense, chanting prayers, and offering food and money to the gods. Family traditions are of utmost importance. Taiwanese people honor and respect their parents according to ancient

Confucian precepts. Many who go abroad to study or work later return to Taiwan to take care of their aging parents. Children stay closely connected with their parents, striving to please them by studying English, music, math, or calligraphy in after-school cram schools called *bushibans*. Conservative habits in dress and behavior dominate everyday life, much to my delight, as the mother of a teenage daughter. Low-cut, skin-revealing Western styles are much less evident on the streets of Taipei.

Traditional Chinese holidays are celebrated with great fervor in Taiwan—Spring Festival, Tomb-Sweeping Day, Mid-Autumn Festival, Moon Festival, and Chinese New Year dot the year with festivities. On holidays, shopkeepers burn stacks of artificial money in front of their shops in offerings to the gods, hoping to ensure their continued prosperity and the well-being of their ancestors.

Restaurants in Taiwan serve perhaps the most authentic Chinese cuisine anywhere, having been spared the excesses of the Cultural Revolution that literally killed the gourmet—a.k.a. bourgeois—cooks. Some of the best cooks in China fled to Taiwan in 1949 and set up shop. Today in Taipei one can find delicious authentic cuisine from each region of China—Sichuan, Canton, Beijing, Shanghai, and Hunan. In addition, Japanese, Vietnamese, Thai, Malaysian, and increasingly Italian, French, and other international cuisines are now found in abundance throughout the vibrant city of Taipei.

Chris and Cara reveled in the life of Taipei and in their new-found independence. Because Taipei is one of the safest cities in the world, we allowed them to explore at will by bus, metro, and taxi. They grew up going with their friends to noodle shops, temples, teahouses, coffee shops, jazz clubs, and alley night markets. With each day's adventure their Chinese language developed and their intercultural confidence grew. There was never a lack of things to do in this city open 24/7, with endless places to discover, either in the little valley of Tienmu, where our life centered, or in Greater Taipei.

Given our one-China policy, with the official U.S. embassy located in Beijing, the United States does not have official diplomatic relations with Taiwan. Jim was assigned as political chief to the "unofficial" American Institute in Taiwan (AIT), an embassy in all but name. At

AIT, he immersed himself in the intricacies of Taiwan politics and society. In Taiwan's thoroughgoing, vibrant democracy, politics are ever present and all consuming. Jim's work was both challenging and interesting, as he sought to learn the various factions in each political party and their stance on the sensitive and strategically dangerous issue of Taiwan independence. With a "Green" (pro-independence) president, Chen Suibian, the relationship between Taiwan and China remained an extremely tense roller-coaster ride through our four years in Taiwan.

We spent evenings with the president and his ministers, where we were able to discuss the pros and cons of Taiwan's independence from mainland China. Although the Taiwanese people are ethnically Chinese, they have a unique history and culture that developed largely separate from China. There is a strong sense of Taiwan pride and a resurgence of the use of Taiwanese language in place of Mandarin. China, on the other hand, has always insisted that Taiwan is part of China and has, on numerous occasions, kept Taiwan in place by threatening invasion. In recent years, China has built up an arsenal of some 1,000 ballistic missiles along its southern coast, aimed at Taiwan. The United States, through its unofficial AIT representation, constantly sought to defuse these cross-straits tensions. As political chief, Jim played a central role in the complex and nuanced trilateral relationship between the United States, Taiwan, and China. His work could not have been more important to regional and global security.

Taiwan is a hybrid of traditional Chinese culture, colonial Japanese culture, and cutting-edge high-tech Asia. Because it was a colony of Japan for fifty years until 1945, many vestiges of Japanese culture are still visible throughout the island. Japanese restaurants are very popular; some of the older people on the island still speak Japanese better than Chinese; and Taiwanese formality and cordiality are more Japanese than mainland Chinese

The numerous "hot spas" found scattered throughout the mountains of Taiwan were among Jim's and my favorite vestiges of Japan. Sitting on the Pacific "Ring of Fire," Taiwan is a volcanic island with innumerable natural sulfur hot springs gurgling from the mountainsides. Driving through certain areas of the island, you see vast columns of white sulfuric steam spewing out of mountain crevices, accompanied by the pungent odor of sulfur, akin to rotten eggs. This smell grew on us after a time, because of its association with wonderful hot baths.

After the Japanese seized Taiwan from China as a colony in 1895, they began to develop the hot springs into baths on the order of those in Japan. After the Japanese left the island in 1945, the Taiwanese continued the tradition, creating a trail of exotic hot spas throughout the island, unlike anywhere else in the world, even Japan itself. Jim and I did not let a week go by without going at least once to soak in a hot spa. The spas range from elegant private rooms overlooking deep green valleys, to outdoor natural pools tucked in forest glens. Sometimes we would take a room with our own spa for several hours of soaking; other times we would go to the public hot spas, where we would separate into the men's and women's public baths and bathe *au naturel* in large steaming pools with Taiwanese bathers. After I got over the initial strangeness of bathing nude, I began to explore all the various *wenquan* (hot springs) on my own. Never did I let a cold dreary rainy Taiwan day get me down; rather, I headed for the mountains and slipped into hot pools of soothing aqua-colored water. There I met Taiwanese people who made me feel welcome, and were so delighted to meet a *waiguoren* (foreigner) who not only spoke Chinese, but also loved the hot spas as much as they did.

One of my favorite spots lay at the bottom of a deep rocky ravine where a hot spring boiled into a rushing mountain stream. I discovered the hot springs one day when, to celebrate my birthday, I invited a few of my friends to spend several days up in the mountains in the Japanese Guest house. Each day we had a different adventure. One day, we set out looking for the perfect hot spa. We hiked through cascading rice paddies, small villages, and down a trail that ran along a river bank, until we stumbled onto a clearing with a series of natural sulfur pools ranging in temperature from egg-boiling hot at the top to ice cold at the bottom. Waterfalls and soaring green mountains enveloped in mist surrounded the layered pools. We felt as though we had arrived in our own mountain Shangri-La! The locals called this *Bayan* (eight smokes) because of the steam rising from the pools. It was an unforgettable birthday, spent laughing and sighing with delight, while bathing in hot pools, as the cool natural waterfalls poured over us and locals wished me *Zhu ni Shengre Kuai Le!* (Happy Birthday). Not a bad way to celebrate life!

From the hot spas, I began to explore every facet of Taiwan— mountain trails, island history, teahouses, puppet and temple dramas, cuisine, Buddhist monasteries, mountain villages, and beaches. Every trip seemed to lead to adventure and a story. I fed these into a monthly column I wrote for the island's English magazine, *Centered on Taipei*. This writing, in turn, gave me a good excuse to see more, learn more, and meet more people, in order to share the richness I discovered in Taiwan with as many people as I could.

Taiwan's mountains are laced with an elaborate network of trails that are well maintained and well traveled by hikers. From our house, it was just a few minutes to the rim of volcanic mountains with stunning views of the northern tip of the island, with the Pacific Ocean to the east and the East China Sea to the northwest. On sunny days, I would head for the mountains in the early morning. Sometimes I was the only person there, surrounded by unbelievable beauty, while millions of people rushed about in the city of Taipei below me. The rolling fields stretched out in all directions, almost resembling the Scottish highlands but ringed here with impressively high, deep green mountains. With our dog Jingles, I reveled in the natural splendor. Jingles would roll ecstatically in the grass, while I shouted at the top of my lungs, thanking my creator for giving me this special place to retreat. In the springtime, calla lilies grew on Yangmingshan in endless fields of white, surrounded by mountains of billowing steam. I would go as often as I could to breathe in the exquisite beauty.

In summer, trekkers with walking sticks and hiking gear fill the trails. The highest mountain, just minutes from our house, was Seven Star Mountain (Qixing Shan). Climbing to the 1,100-meter summit gave one a breathtaking view of the city of Taipei and the northern tip of Taiwan. Hiking up through the sulfur steam, you might encounter monkeys, colorful tropical birds, and highly poisonous snakes. Every person on the trails was friendly and welcoming. In winter, thick mist covered the mountains, making them as mysterious as a Chinese painting, but providing a good excuse to stop off in any of numerous teahouses to sip a cup of hot fragrant mountain tea. Autumn, with its crystal clear skies, flowing waves of long mountain grasses, and cooler air was the most intoxicating of the seasons. Often I would head to the coast, less than forty minutes away, to sit on the beach and watch the waves. What other city has so many magnificent options in such close proximity?

United Airlines *Hemisphere* magazine commissioned me to write an article titled "Three Perfect Days in Taipei." The photographer sent by the magazine to travel around with me and photograph the island exclaimed, "Wow, this is the best-kept secret in all of Asia!" After the article was published and placed in every United Airlines seatback, the Taiwanese Tourist Board thanked me profusely for helping to bring more tourists to Taiwan. I was happy to share my love of Taiwan and hoped it would entice new visitors.

I began consulting with a small firm, Asia Business Communications, founded by three Taiwanese women who had been Citibank vice presidents. My job was to develop training courses for Taiwan business executives in Western-style management skills. I taught courses to Taiwanese people working for IBM, ABM Amro, and other corporations, on Western business negotiating skills, presentation skills, and teleconferencing style. Most of these young executives worked with Western clients, or had a Western home office, and needed to learn about Western business styles and build confidence in their business English. My job was to be sure they understood the directness and efficiency that characterize Western business.

Personally, I had learned much from living in Taiwan. The Eastern ways of personal relationships and Eastern etiquette have much to offer the West. The concept of "saving face" can soften the edges of social interaction. Waiting until a private moment to criticize a colleague rather than doing so in public can be not only kinder but more effective in communicating criticism. Cordiality and hospitality to guests is a grace at which Easterners excel. We in the West would do well to emulate some of this Eastern etiquette in our hectic busy lives. My worldview had grown increasingly influenced by Eastern thinking as I became more deeply immersed in Taiwanese culture, taking *Taiqi* (Chinese shadowboxing) classes, learning about traditional hand puppets and aboriginal art, participating in elegant ancient tea rituals, studying Mandarin, and making Taiwanese friends.

One of the most meaningful trips I made in Taiwan was near the end of my stay there. For several years, I had been meeting with a group of women to explore our spiritual beliefs. We called ourselves "FOG," for Friends of God. For our last meeting, I arranged for us to meet Hsin Tao, a Buddhist monk whom I had interviewed for a story two years earlier. Master Hsin Tao lived in a monastery on an exquisite mountaintop overlooking the Pacific Ocean. He had come from humble beginnings in Burma, moved to Taiwan to join the military, and finally ended up becoming a Buddhist monk.

After seventeen years of meditating, his vision of what he had to do was made clear to him. He decided to build a Museum of World Religions and to bring people of various religious beliefs together to promote understanding. While he was well on his way to realizing this plan, the events of 9/11 solidified his belief that gathering people from the various religions of the world for dialogue was important for world peace. Master Hsin Tao's museum in Taipei houses an unmatched exhibit of artifacts of each of the seven major world religions. By the time we met him, this humble man had traveled and met with most of the world's great religious leaders—the pope, the archbishop of Canterbury, the Dalai Lama, and numerous imams, priests and rabbis. He had set up dialogues between Hindus and Christians, Muslims and Jews, and Buddhists and Muslims. His work was world-renowned, and I felt I was going to meet a peacemaker.

Master Hsin Tao invited us to his monastery for a day of rest and tranquility. Climbing up the mountain to see him, we were not completely certain why we were going. Like the weather that day, we were in a bit of a fog. Once there, we toured the monastery, had tea with one of his disciples, who explained the way the nuns and monks lived, and described the mission of their center. Then we were invited to meet with the master himself. As we sat sipping tea with this congenial, humble man, he taught us how to find peace within through meditation. We asked him how one small person, such as he, could make such a difference in the world. He replied that we must begin within, then "light the light of each person you meet." His simple message had special meaning for me, for this was exactly what my life in each country had been focused on. As we left the monastery the sun was shining brightly over the mountains of Taiwan, and the fog had lifted, both literally and figuratively. As we returned to Taipei, thrilled to have been there, we each felt inspired to follow Master Hsin Tao's simple advice, which had such a profound message.

Although the move from the United States was initially difficult for our family, it reinforced my belief in the value of international experience. It was hard to leave our comfortable life in the United States, but living in Taipei greatly expanded our horizons. All four of us learned to open our hearts and minds to Asia, an Asia that will play an increasingly important role in the world of the future. Asia changed us, making us much more appreciative of differences, more broadminded in our thinking, more aware politically, and more open to the world. We grew to be great admirers of Taiwanese culture, with its cordiality and kindness. After four years living in Taiwan, none of us was ready to return to Washington.

Lucky for us, we returned in the midst of a presidential election in America. A few months after we returned, the country elected Barack Obama—a multicultural, biracial man who had been an expatriate, and believed in diplomacy and in living and working in harmony with the people of all cultures,—the forty-fourth president of the United States.

It was nice to be home!

Epilogue

The More Things Change, the More They Stay the Same

I always wonder whether I will ever go back to the places in which we have lived. Upon leaving a post, I know deep in my heart that the likelihood is no, never; that I am leaving for good and closing the door forever on a chapter of my life.

Once we move on to the next place, I struggle to hold onto the last. Leaving India and moving to Kenya, I felt a sense of panic, when I realized I couldn't remember the faces of our amahs, Jaya and Leela. It felt horrible that they were so rapidly fading from my memory. I tried desperately to remember the aroma of the jasmine in their hair, the color of their saris, and the beauty in their faces.

Each place we have lived seems a complete lifetime, so distinct and different from the last, and so over when we leave. With our Foreign Service lifestyle, these mini-lifetimes are encapsulated in stretches of three short years. There is a cycle to the process. In the first year, all is overwhelming, different, and confusing. The learning curve is steep. By the second year you establish routines, make friends, begin to feel comfortable, start to work and discover how you can make a contribution to the country. By the third year you are well established in the place. People know you. It is your home. You identify with it and are contributing to the society. Then before you know it, you have to move on. Each time, it is heartbreaking.

In 2005, the business I co-founded in India, Global Adjustments, celebrated its tenth anniversary. It was also the tenth anniversary of the American International School of Chennai. As co-founder of both, I was invited back to attend the parallel anniversary ceremonies as the guest of honor! Heretofore, we had never returned to any of our previous posts, and I wondered what it would be like going back to Madras, now called Chennai. I would have loved for Jim, Christopher, and Caroline, my fellow travelers, to have accompanied me, but it turned out that only I was free to make the journey to India from Taiwan.

Arriving at the Chennai Airport brought memories rushing back from deep inside—the lovely, smiling brown faces, the women in colorful saris, the lyrical way Tamils nod their heads, the excruciatingly slow baggage claim, the densely crowded airport arrival area, the stifling hot sultry air, the crazy traffic. Although it had been ten full years since we had left, my senses stirred the memories of my heart.

Walking through the arrival gate, I saw the warm welcoming face of Ranjini, my dear friend and former business partner, dressed in a beautiful flowing crimson sari, a shimmering bindi in the middle of her forehead, waiting with open arms. From that first welcome embrace, Ranjini and I were chatting and sharing ideas as if we had never been apart—our friendship so deep that it took but moments to resume where we had left off ten years before.

Ranjini had arranged every detail of the week with the care of someone who loves her native India and is proud to share it. She had booked a room for me at the grand old Madras Club, adjacent to where we had lived ten years before. Driving through the gate, I experienced a rush of nostalgia and immediately felt at home. Nothing had changed; all was as I had remembered it from the time when we lived there. The whitewashed buildings still needed a fresh coat of paint!

To my astonishment, the bearer who greeted me and took my bags remembered me. "Are you not the Madame from #2 Turnbulls Road with the two small children?"

"Yes, why yes, I am, though my children are now fifteen and twelve years old and we live in Taiwan!" I gushed.

Ranjini left to give me time to rest after my long journey from Taiwan, but I was too excited to sleep. Alone in the twilight, I wandered around the Madras Club, where I had spent so much of my time. It was as if I was allowed to go back and peek at the very places that had etched an indelible memory in my heart, like going back in a time machine. It was all still there—the Adyar River and the jogging track adjacent to the playground where Caroline and Christopher used to play with Jaya. Only now, other aunties were there with a new generation of little children frolicking on the same swings and in the same big sand pit. The great ballroom was decorated for Christmas, with a huge sparkling Christmas tree in the center of the foyer as before, where tiny Caroline and Christopher had received gifts from Santa Claus. I sipped a lime soda on the club terrace almost as if I had never left. In the soft yellow light that washed the trees, I walked quietly around the club, taking in the smells, the calm, and the aura that was for me India.

The next morning at 6 a.m., Ranjini, in her white salwa chemise, knocked on my door and off we went for a walk around the track. As we began our trek, friends, whom I had not seen in ten years, graciously greeted me with a bow of the head and a Tamil "*Vanakkam.*" Most of the faces on the track were familiar, people who had been part of our past life, all still there doing their morning rituals. These members of Madras society, who had been dear friends, still remembered my name and face! I was touched and filled with a twinge of sadness for all we had left behind.

Ranjini left me to eat a delicious breakfast of fresh papaya and mango on the terrace overlooking the Adyar. At a small table set with starched white linens and fine china and silver, the bearer served me with the flair of bygone colonial days. From the club terrace, I could see the gate of our old house and peek just over the garden wall. In my mind's eye, I could see Christopher and Caroline running through the grass chasing our dog, Jingles. Everything at the club seemed frozen in time; even the old-fashioned ladies' room remained as it had been back in the prewar era, when British ladies lounged about powdering their noses and recuperating from the heat. I wandered over to the tennis courts, where Jim and I used to play, to see if anyone I knew was there. Sure enough, my friends Gopi and Comi, who had played every day, were there knocking about in their tennis whites, looking a bit older but still volleying like pros. I sat and watched them play, delighted that my cherished memories still held true, and nothing had changed.

Outside the club, however, not just the name of the city but many other things had changed in Chennai. First and foremost my business, Global Adjustments, had grown to a staff of over forty people, with offices in Chennai, Bangalore, Delhi, Hyderabad, and Mumbai. Its clients were from every major international business in India. The focus of Global Adjustments' work had also changed, from primarily orienting foreigners to Indian life to helping to prepare the "global Indian" to cope with the interdependent global market. Ranjini's vision for the company had been the driving force for innovation and growth. In addition to helping expatriates settle into India, Global Adjustments was now working with Indian business people on "accent neutralization," Western protocol and customs, and communication skills that would help them cope with the new "flat" world.

Entering my old office, I was welcomed by the greatly enlarged staff of ambitious young Indian employees. During a brainstorming session on the future plans for Global Adjustments, I told the staff how incredibly important I feel the work of Global Adjustments is — there may be no more critical work than promoting international understanding among people of different cultures. Since September 11th, our very survival depends upon this.

My former driver, S. Padmanabhan (S.P.), came to the office to greet me. Bearing gifts in gratitude, he told me he now owns a fleet of trucks and is an entrepreneur businessman with many employees working for him. He ships goods all over India. He was so proud, and I was so pleased to have played a small part in enabling him to find success.

The new Chennai has a high-tech sector on Tarimani Road to the south of the city, which has brought hundreds of foreigners to live and work in Chennai. The influx of foreign business also has brought chic new coffee shops, spas, and clothing stores to every street corner. Despite the Western influx, however, most Chennai women hold onto their Indian traditions and still wear saris. Prosperous women now wear designer saris and go to upscale spas for relaxation. Expatriates were so numerous that, sadly, they no longer mingled as much socially with the local Indians as we had, when we lived there with a much smaller population of Westerners. Isolated in the large expatriate community, the new expats experience much less of the gracious hospitality of South Indians than Jim and I had enjoyed.

At the time of my visit, Intel and BMW were just then setting up businesses in Chennai, each bringing more than a billion dollars' worth of business to the city. Ranjini had arranged for me to conduct a workshop on Western culture for savvy Indian high-tech workers. It was apparent that young Indians today are a very different breed from that of previous generations. Smart, educated, and competitive, they are confident that India is on the rise and that Chennai and other cities will continue to benefit.

Also at the time, Jayalalitha, the movie-star-turned-politician, was once again the chief minister of Tamil Nadu. Having survived a series of corruption scandals from her first term when we lived there, she had been reelected. Under her administration, the city's infrastructure had not kept pace with the high-tech development. While I was visiting, the monsoon rains flooded the streets, and people, even women in beautiful saris, still had to slosh through water up to their waists to get home because of poor drainage. Auto rickshaws still zigzagged through the maze of automobiles, scooters, and animal traffic, weaving through mud, sewage, oxcarts and disorder. The power even still went off sporadically at the Madras Club.

The Kapeleswaram Temple in Mylapore, however, was still as magnificent as ever. As I walked barefoot amid the colorful and innumerable Hindu deity icons, throngs of people worshipped as they had for more than a thousand years. A decade earlier, Jim and I had brought our babies to this very spot to witness the worship ceremonies and view the towering, brightly colored, elaborately carved temple.

While parts of India are changing rapidly, other parts remain completely unchanged. As India forges ahead to become a major player in the modern global economy, I hope it never loses the beauty and uniqueness of its culture. When I return to Chennai in another ten years, I hope not to see a sterile, fast-paced Western-style city. And I hope that Indians will still be doing their daily pujas (worship) at their neighborhood temples, will still be wearing vibrant colors and eating delicious spicy foods with their hands, and will always smile with the natural grace that is the charm of

South India. It is this India that Global Adjustments takes pride in sharing with the rest of the world.

Differences are what make the world interesting. Returning to Madras after ten years, I found the city thriving. And yet I was happy to see the people maintaining the traditions that make it dear to my heart. In the 1990s, when we lived there, I had felt a sense of regret that I had not been able to work with the poor people or contribute in some way to the alleviation of poverty. Going back ten years later to celebrate the success of Global Adjustments, I realized that this company had made it possible for many foreign businesses to move to Chennai and set up shop. The American International School of Chennai, which I had helped to create, provided foreigners a place for their children to study in an international atmosphere. These two organizations had played a major role in facilitating foreign investment and growth in Chennai. I would like to think that this influx of investment had improved the lives of even Chennai's street people in small ways.

As my driver approached the gate of the huge new ten-million-dollar red brick American International School of Chennai, my thoughts went back to the school's humble beginnings, with our first eighteen students marching into rented rooms in the Russian Cultural Center. As I walked through the hallways and saw the children laughing and talking, I knew it was well worth the work of starting the school. Walking into a first grade classroom, Becky Thomas, the first teacher we had hired in 1996, warmly greeted me. Despite the many changes that we had both seen, she had the same warm smile and sparkling eyes that greeted my son Christopher on his first day in kindergarten. Now I was being welcomed as the co-founder to a school of four hundred fifty children. (Since my visit the school has grown to over 700 students.) As I met one of Becky's first grade students, she exclaimed, "I have never met a real founder before. I thought they were usually hung on the wall!"

On the evening of the Global Adjustments Gala 10th Anniversary Celebration, I dressed in a red Chinese *qipao* from Taiwan. As I entered the ballroom of the Park Sheraton Hotel and greeted the more than 500 guests, I could barely refrain from crying. With all the women in gorgeous saris, and men in white Indian shirts, I stood out in my Chinese outfit. Yet, I was a part of the success that was Global Adjustments and a part of the city of Chennai.

After watching many presentations about the exciting and far-reaching work of Global Adjustments, I was called on stage to speak. I praised Ranjini for her vision and her outstanding leadership of Global Adjustments over the last ten years. Then I quoted the late Mahatma Gandhi, who said, "You must be the change you want to see in the world!"

Ranjini mounted the stage and presented me with a plaque that, serendipitously, read in bold letters,

To our founder and the raison d'être *of Global Adjustments*
"You must be the change you want to see in the world."

And that is what we continue to try to be.

Postscript
Nothing Stands Still

We decided that our children, especially Christopher, who was "made in China," ought to see China before we left Taiwan. So for their spring break from Taipei American School in April 2007, we arranged a trip to Beijing, Xian, Shanghai, and Hong Kong. To add to the fun, I booked us in the Jianguo Hotel in Beijing, the hotel in which Jim and I first lived nineteen years earlier, when we landed in China as newlyweds on our first Foreign Service posting. Christopher, who had left China when he was eleven months old, was now in the eleventh grade in high school, 6'2" tall, and with a growing command of spoken Chinese *Putonghua* (standard Chinese). We wanted to show Christopher and Caroline some of our history, and I was hoping to clarify mine.

Upon arriving at the airport in Beijing, I was extremely conscious of the feelings I had had the first time I landed there in 1988. Then, I was afraid, claustrophobic, and ready to flee home. In fact, it had been the shock of my life to realize what I had done by marrying Jim and letting my life be swept up in the whirlwind of the Foreign Service. Now, after twenty years of marriage, how did I look back on my choices? As we drove into the city of Beijing, the city was much larger and more developed, but the air was thick and enveloped in yellow dust and mist. The ride into the city felt reminiscently eerie, tapping into some of that old loneliness I had experienced so many years before.

Even Caroline felt the strangeness of it and said to me, "How could you have lived here all those years?" I wondered myself and yet knew in some visceral way that our first China experience had permanently marked my character, forced me to face life's existential quality, and allowed me to find out who I was.

As we entered the lobby of the Jianguo Fandian (hotel), memories came pouring back. Little had changed. Though the hotel had been renovated to keep up with the modernization of Beijing, the rooms, the lobby, and the restaurants were basically the same ones in which we had moved around for our first four months living there in 1988. It actually felt a bit like home—comfortable and safe.

When we woke the next morning, the sun was shining and Beijing had a new quality of lightness and energy. Looking out our bedroom window into the alley behind, I saw the same houses that I remembered, with laundry hanging out in the bright but chilly Beijing sun and bicycles parked in front of each apartment. But, as we walked out of the hotel, I realized that this was not the Beijing I had left in 1991. Gone were the stacks of white cabbage to help people get through the harsh winter. This was a new city aggressively on the move. Gone was the bicycle traffic. Instead there were thousands of cars now, with few of the motorcycles we had in Taipei. Ring roads encircled the city. When we had lived there before, they had just completed the Second Ring Road. Now, six ring roads went out concentrically in ever-larger diameters from the city, the largest running 160 kilometers around Beijing.

World-class hotels filled the Jianguomenwai area, where most of the foreign community lived in 1988, and even the old apartment buildings for foreigners had been sandblasted to look extremely clean and well built. Jim and I could hardly believe the changes— this poor, backward city had transformed itself into a metropolis of innovative architecture, vast neon tableaus, and obviously wealthy people. My mind flashed back to the days when PLA soldiers had lined the streets after the Tiananmen massacre and kept the Chinese people from interacting with foreigners. Now people in Beijing walked with purpose. No longer wearing blue Mao jackets, instead they sported the latest fashions and freely mingled with tourists from all over the world.

As we rode into Tiananmen Square, we spoke with our taxi driver about the events of June 4th, 1989. He openly discussed the Tiananmen massacre and talked about how his government had *sha ren* (killed people) there. I could not believe how unafraid he was to speak about that event. When we lived there, no one dared utter a word about what happened in Tiananmen Square without fear of being arrested. For many of the young people in Beijing in 2007, that event was ancient history they knew or cared little about. People strolled about and laughed in the square, taking photos of one another and of us, seemingly oblivious to the awful history of that night. Most *Beijingren* (Beijing people) seem, in fact, quite happy with their lives, proud of the progress of their nation, and looking hopefully to the future. Their sense of national pride was palpable.

We walked across the full length of Tiananmen Square, from Qianmen Gate, past Mao's tomb and the Great Hall of the People. Then, Jim animatedly told our children about the events of June 4, 1989—where he had stood when he witnessed the killings that night, where the students led their mass democracy rallies, where Dan Rather broadcast live, where Gorbachev arrived, where Zhao Ziyong had apologized and warned the students to leave the Square, where the tanks came from, where our car was parked through the whole thing, where the people had burned an armored personnel carrier. Like today's modern Beijing youth, however, our children found these stories of twenty years ago only remotely interesting. They were thinking about patronizing the huge Kentucky Fried Chicken outlet on the square. Jim and I, on the other hand, were in awe at the normality of the place where such a major moment in history had occurred, one in which we had participated and could never forget.

We drove past the Chinese Women's Federation, now housed in an elegant building right on Jianguo Boulevard, the main road east of the square. When I worked with them in 1990 to organize a Sino-American Women's Conference, they had been located in an old factory-like building on a back street. Hosting our Sino-American Conference was practice for their hosting of the United Nations International Women's Conference in 1995, which obviously brought them into the mainstream of Chinese consciousness. Now their building stands prominently on the major street in town, alongside the most elegant hotels and government buildings.

We wandered through room after room of the Imperial Forbidden City, attempting to explain the Song, Ming, and Qing dynasties to our children, while gazing at the beautifully cantilevered classical rooftops and the huge expanse of public space. The most notable thing about the Forbidden City is that its 9,999 rooms contain very little. Most of the treasures remaining in the city at the end of the imperial rule in 1911, when the palace was opened to the public, are now exhibited in the National Palace Museum in Taipei, where I was then working as an English docent. The knowledge of all that happened in the Forbidden City and the saga of those beautiful pieces of art made the walk through it all the more poignant for me. My expanded knowledge of Chinese history, acquired at Taipei's Palace Museum, provided a thread of continuity in my life for my return to this empty but magnificent Forbidden City, where I once roamed with Christopher when he was a tiny baby. Of far greater interest to Caroline and Christopher was the Starbuck's café, tucked remarkably into a far corner of the ancient Forbidden City, a reminder of the openness to capitalism in this communist country. The cafe provided us a nice reprieve from the cold Beijing March air.

Leaving the Forbidden City, we rambled among the lakes behind it, first Bei Hai (north sea), where Jim and I loved to ice skate in winter, and then to Qian Hai and Hou Hai (front and back lakes). What was once an area of innumerable small alleys, or *hutongs*, full of traditional old courtyard houses, where Jim and I would ride our Flying Pigeon bicycles along with Beijingers, has now become a tourist attraction replete with wine bars, souvenir shops, and cafes along the lakefront. Though charming and burgeoning with tourists, the area has become a bit like a museum. We rented a pedicab, which carried us through these ancient *hutongs*—now turned into tourist sites—the only relics remaining of old Beijing. As we chatted with our pedicab driver, we found that despite the influx of money and wealth in Beijing, he made just 60 yuan (about US$7) a month. The rest of his takings went to his *laoban* (boss). This was the third time in our first day in Beijing that we encountered the layers and layers of money-handling. It was quite obvious that along with the rise of capitalism had come mafia-like criminal gangs, prostitution, begging, theft, and many other vices. As Deng Xiaoping, in attempting to keep out the more unsavory elements of the bourgeoisie, had put it, "When you open the windows, the flies will come in." Sure enough, despite the remarkable progress under capitalism, the flies are swarming in Beijing and other Chinese cities.

Still, China was undeniably on the move. Its airports were sparkling, new, and ready for the Olympics in 2008. In a move to make China greener, the government had planted countless thousands of trees along the roadsides to hold down the dust from the Gobi desert. The long-term urban planning was truly impressive.

We took our children to the obligatory tourist spots—the Great Wall, where I once held Christopher in a snuggly, the Ming tombs, where we used to picnic, and the beautiful Summer Palace of the Empress Dowager, a remnant from the declining days of the Empire. These visits gave us a perfect time to discuss some of China's long and complicated history. The children, however, preferred shopping in the Silk Alley, once a black market alley full of export items, now converted into a six-floor mall. Caroline became quite adept at bargaining for deals, picking up some putative designer clothes to take home with her.

Every street billboard we saw promoted the 2008 Olympics in Beijing. Most impressive for me was that there were going to be Olympic events for athletes with disabilities. After the years I had worked with the Disabled People's Federation in Beijing, promoting sports and arts with disabled children, it was rewarding to see that people with disabilities were now being included in the major events of the international Olympics. Ramps and handicap access were now apparent in many of the new buildings in Beijing, and sign language appeared in a small inset box during announcements and programs broadcast on television. It made me smile to remember how I had taught the staff of the Chinese Disabled People's Federation how to sing English songs in sign language, and how we debated the importance of allowing deaf people to sign rather than forcing them to lip-read. Now sign language was included on most television programs and in airplane emergency announcements.

Back at the hotel, I inquired at Justine's, the hotel's French restaurant, whether a man named Mr. Li still worked there as a chef. When we had lived in Beijing, Li had cooked for us at our home during his off hours. I knew it was a long shot that he might still be working at the hotel, but I had always wondered what happened to him. The maître d' said there were two Mr. Li's working at the hotel, one around thirty years of age and the other around forty-five. Since our Mr. Li had worked with us sixteen years before, I told the maître d' it was probably the latter whom I had known. During breakfast in the hotel the following morning, Mr. Li, our wonderful cook from so many years before, passed the picture window and waved in at me. He was indeed the same man. Years before, while preparing delicious French dishes for us while I fed baby Christopher in his high chair, Mr. Li taught him Chinese words. He would call Christopher by his Chinese name, Guifeng (precious wind), and tell him the words for everything in the kitchen. Mr. Li met sixteen-year-old Guifeng, who could now carry on a conversation with him in Chinese. That night Mr. Li took us all out for a banquet of Peking duck and other Beijing delicacies, and over Beijing *pijiu* (beer) we reminisced about the Beijing of old and the good times we had.

Realizing the major role China will undoubtedly play in the future, Christopher was considering taking a gap year in China between high school and college to study intensive Mandarin. Since he was interested in going to Beijing University, or Beida, we decided to visit the school. Beida was one of the centers where the student movement sprang up in April 1989, and where Jim and I used to go at night to listen to students publicly debate democracy and human rights. Today, Beida has many elegant new buildings. Clearly the Chinese government is investing in the university to make it one of the premier universities in the world, eventually to rival Harvard, Yale, Oxford, and Cambridge.

While our days were spent in the burgeoning cities of China, my dreams at night were of my early life with Jim in the old, pre–building boom China. One day Jim and I took an evening stroll past the U.S. Embassy to Ritan Park, where I used to practice *Taiqi* each morning. Once ringed by rifle-toting teenaged People's Liberation Army soldiers standing at guard following the Tiananmen massacre, the Embassy is now barricaded behind walls and fences to protect it from terrorists. We tried to find the Ritan Park Restaurant, where we had enjoyed many evenings eating dumplings (*jiaozi*) and drinking *pijiu*. To our disappointment, we found only a chic upscale restaurant with elaborate traditional Chinese décor and an expensive menu. Not all changes are necessarily for the better. We longed for the days when the clatter of the restaurant added to the taste of the meal and when there was nothing quite as perfect as a simple bowl of beef noodles or dumplings under the evening sky.

After Beijing, we took the children to see the Tang Dynasty capital of Xian, where the vast tomb of the first emperor, Shi Huangdi, is located. Since the discovery in 1975 of this underground wonder from 2,200 years ago, thousands of visitors have come to see the great underground army of terra cotta soldiers guarding the Emperor's tomb. Fortuitously, the aged farmer who made the original discovery came in while we were visiting, and we were able to talk with him. In his eighties, he is honored nationwide for his contribution to history. His discovery is an amazing tale and one that almost did not happen.

Obsessed with dying, the first emperor had used some 700,000 slaves to build an underground kingdom to enable him to survive death. The horror of the story is that once the construction was complete, he killed all of the slaves who had worked for decades to build his tomb and its thousands of figures, burying them alive to keep the secret of his amazing army of terra cotta soldiers.

As with Beijing, Xian is another city on the move. The ancient Tang Dynasty capital is developing tourist villages and renovating its Tang treasures to attract visitors from around the world. From a dusty shell of a city in 1975, it has evolved into a dynamic and historic city and a must on any tourist itinerary.

Our last stop on this return journey to China was Shanghai, the city that captivated Jim so much that he wrote his Ph.D. dissertation on the Shanghai of the 1920s and the part it played in the communist rebellion. This has always been a city for foreigners. Once an enclave of colonialists, who excluded Chinese people from much of the city, it is today a modern world-class city the likes of New York or Hong Kong. The Shanghai we visited in the late 1980s was frozen in the 1930s. The Shanghai of 2007, however, had become a cutting-edge world metropolis. Tens of thousands of high-rise buildings had been constructed in the preceding decade

On our first night in Shanghai, we took the children to see the old Peace Hotel to give them a taste of 1930s Shanghai. We dined on the top floor overlooking the Bund, while Jim, wearing his historian's hat, gave them a long history lesson over dinner, covering the remarkable events in Shanghai since the Opium War in the mid-nineteenth century. After wandering through the Old City and having tea at the ancient teahouse in the middle of the insular Yuanyuan Garden Lake, we walked down Nanjing Road past modern shopping malls and glitzy shops. While the government may still be Communist, the economy is booming with colorful capitalism. On our last night in Shanghai, we crossed the Wangpu River from the Bund to Pudong and dined high on the 89th floor of the Jinmao Tower in the Grand Hyatt Hotel, whose magnificent atrium lobby soars upward from the 56th floor to the top floor! In 1989, there had been nothing taller than two-story warehouses in Pudong. Now the skyscrapers on what used to be a soggy mudflat soared ninety floors and higher.

As we shuttled on the 230-miles-per-hour Maglev train to the vast new Pudong International Airport, we could hardly believe our eyes. So much had changed in such a short time.

The past was just a memory, and the future seemed unlimited.

As I looked at Jim, I realized that without him I would not have lived through the history of Tiananmen Square or seen the old China. I would never have learned to speak Chinese or met so many people who have changed my life. I realized then and there, it had all been worth it. The richness of our lives was beyond measure. The most remarkable sensation for me was that nothing stands still, things constantly change, and the past gets buried by the present. Sadly, unless someone is willing to keep and share the stories, they are lost forever. Perhaps that is why I wrote this book.

Because I have personally been part of the history of each place we have lived and have experienced life-changing events, I have tried to teach my children and many others about the world In addition, I have tried to plant seeds to grow and develop in each place and perhaps in some small way shove our human evolution forward a bit. I benefit from and share all that I have learned, enjoying and contributing to the rich multicultural global society that is emerging more and more each day. History surrounds us, and as Shakespeare so eloquently said, we each "play our part upon the stage." I have thoroughly enjoyed and will continue to enjoy the process of playing mine, welcoming each new adventure as it unfolds. For it is through striving to understand each other that we will thrive and survive on this earth.

"Let there be peace on earth, and let it begin with me."

Index

Breinigsville, PA USA
15 August 2010
243630BV00002B/2/P